Better Homes

HOUSE PLANTS

Edited by Leslie Johns

COLLINS LONDON AND GLASGOW

Orange clivia . . . related to the amaryllis

Contents

Spring bulbs feature in an indoor group

Introduction

This book is for everyone who likes having plants about the house. You will find in it advice and information that will be of great use to both the novice and expert. The pictures and text are carefully chosen and related to help and enable all plant growers to pick the right plants and display them to best advantage.

This book will be of special value to all those who think there is some mystery about growing house plants. All who feel this will be reassured by the advice they will find in this book. Anyone who follows the basic instructions that are contained in the text and pictures is assured of success and can join the ranks of the experts.

The brilliant pictures throughout the book will give many new ideas about plants you would like to grow and also many valuable tips on how to display them. If you adapt the ideas you see, it will help you to make your house glow with colour and interest every day of the year. This is the real beauty of growing house plants. You can use them to anticipate spring or to prolong the memories of the summer that is now over.

If you use this book in this way you will have given yourself an added pleasure in life and made your home a gayer and more gracious place.

CHAPTER 1

The decorative use of house plants

All indoor plants can ornament the rooms you live in. You may enjoy the pleasure of growing them but you can increase this pleasure by selecting and placing plants where they will be the finishing touch that completes an effective decorating plan.

There are usually two major considerations. You may look firstly for boldness of form or leaf, or you may think mainly in terms of colour. Whatever you have in mind you can find a house plant that will embellish your room, fit in with your decoration and grow happily in the conditions of light and warmth that you can provide.

Another factor that you will have to bear in mind is whether the size and style of a particular room deserves a group of plants to make an impressive display or whether you want to single out one particular favourite and make it the focus of interest in a strategic position.

The size of your wall will also affect this. A big plain wall is better suited to a massed display than a small wall area which often serves best for the single plant. In the pages that follow you will find a treasury of ideas to help you create the effect best suited to your home. The main thing to bear in mind is to decide on the effect you want and then choose the plants that will most easily create it for you.

Contrast shapes and colours for effect

Young plants of *Fatsia japonica* with their large palmate leaves complement in colour and shape the tiny red flowers of the kalanchoes. From above hang the trailing shoots of *Philodendron scandens*.

Grouped plants have a greater appeal in the right setting

The mass effect of a handsome group of plants satisfies a universal love of the spectacular. Any one plant in the group may be attractive in its own right, though it is possible to overlook it alone. Put several together in the right setting and you just can't ignore their presence.

There is more than one way to group plants. Pairing them is often just what you want. A collection of many varieties gives the same pleasure as looking into a florists shop. On the following pages you will see these and more ideas for achieving the mass effect.

Choose plants according to their setting

To display a group of plants effectively, you need enough space to avoid overcrowding. If the plants contain a sharp colour contrast, you will require a neutral setting. Against a vivid background, substitute plants with lots of white in their foliage and flowers, or try the wide range of greens which only foliage plants offer.

Look for contrasts of colour, texture and form

Some plants have shiny foliage whereas others have a furry or velvety finish to their leaves. You can choose from large pointed leaves as well as rounded. pierced or lacelike ones. And the green tones vary from palest chartreuse to almost black.

Vary your sizes by combining short ones with taller ones. Place the taller ones towards the back, shorter ones in front, so that all the plants can be seen to best advantage.

Try combining yellow bunch-flowering chrysanthemums which are made to look even more effective when backed by a good dieffenbachia. African violets will appear still daintier when they are backed by a rugged succulent. Ferns look like green lace when contrasted with the solid foliage of big-leaved philodendrons or rubber plants.

Brighten up a dull corner with a colourful display of indoor plants. Place large bushy plants at the rear and small more delicate ones in front. Fill in empty spaces with potted ferns and ivy.

Trolley substitutes for a window ledge

Pink azaleas, pink and white hyacinths, red and white tulips, yellow daffodils, plus some African violets make a gorgeous colour load for a tea trolley that is easy to wheel to other positions. In full bloom, these plants last longer out of the sun.

A room that is furnished with neutral tones can be transformed by a variety of flowers of contrasting colours. A window garden full of bright flowering plants can lift one out of a state of depression during those dreary winter months.

Poinsettias, azaleas, and cyclamen plants must be bought from the florist unless you have your own greenhouse. They will keep considerably longer than most cut flowers, but will not last forever.

Some plants such as African violets and the everblooming begonias will thrive throughout the year under average home conditions. Or it is possible to force your own supply of spring-flowering bulbs for a succession of colourful blooms indoors.

Mix flowering and foliage plants

A few flowering plants will look more impressive if they are combined with foliage plants. Your arrangement will also cover a larger area if grouped with greenery.

The arrangement across the page is a good example of how you can stretch the effect with foliage. Pink cyclamen, yellow and white azaleas, and red poinsettia are the only plants bought as seasonal highlights. You can double the effect of pink and purple violets if they are combined with several varieties of foliage begonias and other plants.

Later chapters will tell you more about the right growing conditions for all the plants pictured here. Check individual requirements for light, water and warmth to make sure the plants you want to combine will stay healthy and retain their good appearance in your window garden.

◀*Early spring from a window sill*

It is easy to force tulips and daffodils for an early indoor spring. Plant bulbs in clay pots and sink them outdoors in the autumn. Bring them indoors during a mild spell where they will bloom weeks earlier than their outdoor cousins.

A window garden brightens up any room

A colourful grouping   Azaleas, poinsettia and cyclamen move in with the foliage plants to brighten a winter window garden.

Flowering plants provide strong colour accents

If you like the dramatic emphasis that a flowering plant gives to a decorating scheme, plan ahead for it! Of course, you can buy beautiful seasonal flowering plants from your florist, and some can't be grown successfully except under greenhouse conditions. There are many varieties, however, which you can grow yourself.

In autumn, you can lift and pot the late-flowering garden plants, chrysanthemums for example, and bring them into the house to be enjoyed after frost. When faded, replace them in the garden if the soil is not frozen. Otherwise tie a plastic bag around the pot and store in a cool, dark spot until spring.

In autumn you can also plant spring bulbs in pots, sink them outdoors and bring them inside for brilliant colour accents long before the garden varieties have pushed their way through the winter-bound earth.

How to make blooms last

When you buy flowering plants from your florist, look for those which are full of buds. Thus you will have the pleasure of watching them swell and open, and it will be longer before they begin to wither.

You must make sure that your plants have enough water as moisture is very important for the production of flowers. If you let the plant become completely dry at this time, the flower buds may be damaged so severely that they will never open.

In bitter winter weather, move the plants away from the window at night if there is danger of their being frost bitten or give them protection against the cold by drawing the curtains or slipping a piece of heavy cardboard between the plants and the windowpane.

◄*Gay flowers brighten winter*

Tulips, both double and single, and daffodils are easy to force for indoor blooms. Azaleas are miniature shrubs, handled by florists who offer reds (as here), pale pinks and whites. Choose a colour that does the most to enhance your room scheme.

Chrysanthemums and a begonia

Big splashes of yellow chrysanthemums create an illusion of sunshine. Pot up your garden variety or buy some from your florist. Other colours usually available are bronze-red, lavender and white. They bring you several weeks of easily obtainable colour.

Showcases for indoor gardens

Take advice from jewellers who know how to display their stones effectively, in brightly lit windows. Plants, too, sparkle when they're set against a window. Colours are enhanced by the extra light, which is also good for plant growth.

A window garden can be part of the architecture, as pictured across the page; or it can be assembled on plant stands and in plant boxes, as shown in the group of sketches you see below. Your window garden should be planned around the window with the most favourable outlook.

The most successful window garden is one that suits the plants with regard to light, temperature and water. If you have a suitable south window, you can grow almost any house plant. East and west windows get enough sun to please some of the most attractive members of the foliage plant family.

◄ Twin stands for a bay window

A pair of plant stands can put a garden in a bay window. Moveable arms accommodate large or small pots of ivies, begonias, ferns, chlorophytum, African violets. Use saucers under plants to avoid stains.

Tiered tables occupy little space ►

Use a tiered table, tea trolley, or a library step table to get this effect. Give a dish garden the top position. Below, set small dracaenas, striped peperomias, grape ivies and African violets or gloxinias in a variety of colours.

◄ A radiator top is adaptable

With a layer of insulation as protection (shingles will do) you can grow many warmth-loving plants on a radiator top. Keep an air space open above the radiator grille so air can circulate.

In the central position is an aquarium (its glass sides trap moist air) planted with coleus, dieffenbachia and African violets. Sansevieria and succulents in flanking plant boxes tolerate drier air.

An indoor-outdoor window garden

This window garden in two parts—inside and outside—is well worth planning for if you're about to build or remodel your home.

Evergreens fill the outdoor half, while the inner half blazes with flowering bulbs backed by luxuriant peppermint geraniums, a spotted dieffenbachia, and climbing grape ivy.

The sketch on the right shows deep gravel layer for drainage. The inside ledge is at a correct working height and the window faces south.

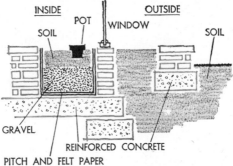

*Display your potted
plants without fear
of watermarks*

By setting your clay pots into waterproof
jardinieres or by adopting one of the pro-
tectors which are sketched below, you can
safeguard against stains on the floor
from spilled water. Place large, difficult-
to-move plants like palms and monstera
pictured above on platforms equipped
with casters. You can then shift them
easily to other places without danger to
you or the plant. The bigger potted plants
look better placed in a corner away from
the house traffic.

GLASSPLATE

ALUMINUM
FOIL

VARNISHED
CLAY SAUCER

LARGE TRAY WITH SEVERAL
POTTED PLANTS

PLATFORM ON CASTERS

Add beauty with potted plants

You can add freshness to any room instantly with a group of potted plants. Their contrasting colours, and dramatic looks have a decorative touch that is hard to equal.

For a big splash of colour, group several potted plants in one spot. Do this with a few big ones like the chrysanthemums across the page. Or use many small pots, inside a dish, tray, or other container, like the coleus you see below in the brass tub.

Be practical in the way you display potted plants, and protect your carpets and furniture against spilled water. The easiest ways of doing this are shown in the sketches below.

Do not expect potted plants to stay decorative forever. Some, like coleus, can be re-rooted from tip cuttings when they become spindly and unattractive.

Others, like potted chrysanthemums, fade and must be removed promptly when they do. If they are a hardy winter variety, you can set them out in your garden. Otherwise, be ruthless about discarding them when they have passed their prime.

Coleus as a set-piece

Coleus (an old favourite because it is so easy to grow from cuttings) is given new sophistication in this setting.

Leave the plants in their pots, spread a layer of vermiculite or coarse sand in a large, moistureproof container. Tilt the outer pots so that foliage falls well over the sides. Keep vermiculite or gravel wet, and the plants in a good, strong light.

SET POTS IN SAND

TILT OUTER POTS

More ideas for colour in winter

Amaryllis, philodendron and azalea can be suitably arranged together

Amaryllis grow from large bulbs and are seemingly without a fixed time-table. If you like surprises, then amaryllis with huge trumpets of red, pink or salmon are for you.

Cold-treated bulbs will bloom indoors in time for Christmas. See the chapter on flowering plants for directions on how to grow amaryllis and how to care for the bulbs after they bloom so that they will be ready to perform again the following year.

It is a pure luxury but an exciting experience to have a real orchid plant

Once they have budded, cattleya orchid plants are fairly strong. Blooms will last for weeks if they are kept in good light and out of the sun.

Only if you supply greenhouse conditions of warmth and humidity will they bloom again.

Colourful companions are small forms of the Rex begonia.

◀ *A burst of colour in a built-in window garden brightens winter*

Summer does not seem so far away when you have put the colour of real flowers into winter days.

This floor-level garden has a paving slab base. It could be adapted to an older house by using a water-proof metal or plastic tray to hold damp sand or shingle.

Admire these plants at close range

Setting is important for small plants, especially those with striking foliage patterns or delicate blooms. Give them attention by placing them on a table so they can be enjoyed at close range.

There are many fine plants that warrant a close look. Those illustrated are foliage begonias, African violets, and white cyclamen. Among others to be appreciated in a similar setting are gloxinias, bushy specimens of the everblooming begonia, and the medium-size spring flowering bulbs such as hyacinths or crocus in yellows, purples and white.

In the foliage family, try a Prayer Plant with pretty, chocolate-brown spots on its leaves, red- or white-veined fittonia, the boldly striped aphelandra, coleus in bright striped hues, and several of the peperomias.

Put the pots into decorative containers to protect table tops and merge with the style of the room.

For a special effect try new combinations

There is an elegant simplicity about both these plants that makes them a good pair for step-table shelves.

Snowy-white blooms of cyclamen look even more picturesque next to the polished heart-shaped leaves of a foliage begonia plant. Set the cyclamen in the sun for a few hours daily to prolong bloom.

Begonias make a ▶ colourful display

Begonias are for north-windows and other spots not in direct sun.

The two in the foreground are in the Rex group. The third plant, with rich, red-leather undersides and a satiny top is a hybrid.

You can easily fit begonias into a room by changing their containers to suit the furniture and decor.

African violets are worth close attention

Planted in a wire basket lined with moisture-holding sphagnum moss are nine African violets, in assorted colours. The basket is set on a metal tray to protect the table.

This is an attractive way to display these young plants that are easily propagated from leaves.

A bold foliage plant

Anyone with a flair for interior decoration can appreciate the part played by a large foliage plant in the right setting. And as a living, growing decoration, it is doubly interesting.

The vertical lines of a big rubber plant break the predominance of horizontals and make a good contrast.

In the room below a pair of cool, white caladium plants, which have big leaves veined in green, introduce freshness and contrast to a warm decorating scheme.

Notice the wide variety of foliage plants shown on the following pages, which are big enough and striking enough to serve as focal points in well-decorated rooms.

Many of these plants will grow well in badly lit situations. Others need more sun. Remembering that they are living things, choose the varieties that will remain healthy and good-looking, and will continue to grow under the room conditions you can offer.

The fancyleaf caladium is a tuberous plant

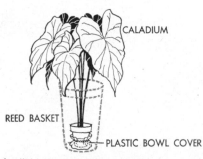

CALADIUM

REED BASKET

PLASTIC BOWL COVER

Available in many colours, some fancyleaf caladiums have pale pink or deeper rose marbling on their green leaves, which will fit another colour scheme.

Caladiums die down to tubers in winter and like very warm humid conditions in the home.

For an attractive display of plants, you can adapt the idea sketched above.

Indiarubber tree ▶ is adaptable to home conditions

One of the most common plants is the rubber plant or ficus. This plant withstands poor conditions of light, temperature, and moisture. It grows best in bright light or shade but not sun.

As this is a big plant it requires a stout container. Here is an opportunity to use something that will blend in with the furniture in the room.

makes an outstanding room accent

One big, green plant looks extravagant

Make a moss stick for growing your climbing plants

A moss stick will supply the moist surface for growing a 'totem pole' scindapsus. See Chapter 2 for directions on how to make your own moss stick.

Monstera has a majestic appearance

Aristocratic monstera is a native of South America. Another climbing plant, it adapts itself surprisingly well to home growing conditions, tolerating any exposure but direct sun. It grows best in a moist atmosphere.

◀ Dieffenbachia has upright foliage

Young plants of this dieffenbachia make fine specimens to display singly. Older plants become spindly but are still good for backgrounds. They can be revitalised by the process of air-layering.

Your moss stick displays graceful foliage

Scindapsus aureus Marble Queen is slower growing than the similar *Philodendron scandens* which also does well on a moss stick. If the stick is kept moist it helps supply the humidity which both need for a healthy growth.

Bold plants for a man's office

If a man has any interest in plants it is possible that he will welcome one to decorate his office. Plants make offices look less austere without being fussy. Choose one that requires little attention and will stand up to the adverse conditions that often prevail. Low light and humidity are common in offices but there are plants that can tolerate these handicaps, and continue to grow and stay attractive over a relatively long period of time.

Because growth will almost certainly be slow, it is best to select a mature plant that looks good from the start.

A foliage plant is your best choice for an office or study, both because it can

One cause of failure with indoor planters is insufficient bottom drainage. As a precaution, leave plants in their own pots and raise to desired height with wood blocks.

Dieffenbachia, monstera and *Philodendron scandens* in a planter are all impressive in size and tolerate reduced light reasonably well. Placing the pots in a bed of gravel is another solution.

For healthier plants, put a lamp near a plant box to supplement daylight

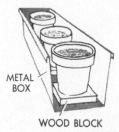

METAL BOX

WOOD BLOCK

Easily grown and colourful plants

Rhoeo discolor, 'Moses-in-a-boat', has odd leaves which are green above and bright purple below. It tolerates low light for rather prolonged periods, but needs frequent watering.

survive with less light than most of the flowering varieties, and because it looks more like a man's choice. Also, it is interesting all year long, not just when in bloom.

Strong leaf outlines rather than fine or lacy ones are best. The philodendron family, several varieties of begonia, dieffenbachia, fiddleleaf fig and rubber plants are all good in this respect.

For greatest appeal, keep a scale in mind. Choose a plant that is small enough or big enough to suit its setting. For a desk top, you'll want one of lesser proportions than those which decorate a big area.

Sit large specimens in tubs, on the floor, making sure thay have enough space to prevent them looking overcrowded or being damaged by passing traffic.

Well-chosen containers also enhance the plants.

Look for colours and shapes that complement both the plant and the decorating scheme of the office. The style of a container, too, should harmonise with the room whether it be Contemporary or Traditional.

A rugged plant for a man's office or study

Fiddleleaf fig is a tall-growing plant with a handsome form. If it is placed away from the direct light, it will need placing in the window sill to catch the sun from time to time. Dust the leaves with a damp cloth.

The schefflera plant makes an attractive display

This plant survives well in badly lit situations. Its crisp, glossy foliage and good appearance make it universally appealing.

Do not overwater or the plant will suffer from leaf drop.

Plants that suit masculine tastes

It is fun watching small plants grow

The pick-a-back plant (*Tolmeia menziesi*) gets its common name from its way of producing new plants at the base of old leaves, so that they appear to be riding on the back of the mother plant. This plant is easy to propagate; simply pin the old leaf to the soil until new roots appear.

A smaller plant can give a big effect ▶

Young plants of Rex begonias have gem-like tones of violet and blue-reds mixed with green that fit subtly into almost any decorating scheme. They make a good choice for an office since they do not like direct sun, and do well in reduced light situations over a long time.

Once a man discovers the cheer, colour and freshness that pot plants can contribute to his private office or study he will always want them on hand. For a few shillings, nothing does more to boost the morale or smarten the decor.

Not every plant is suited to office life, if it is characterised by poor light, bad ventilation or overheating. But there are a number that can withstand poor conditions for fairly long periods, and many which are inexpensive enough to replace when the old ones lose their good appearance.

On these pages we show you examples of that kind of plant. They are foliage plants worth cultivating and are graceful without being so dainty as to look out-of-place in a man's world.

Plants in offices

Do not think that every plant has to be placed in a window. In many offices this is impossible in any case because of heaters and ventilators installed beneath them.

A lamp near a plant will do much to boost the light supply, and will give it a more dramatic setting at the same time.

Plants look well on desks, bookcases, storage cabinets, or on the floor, provided they are big enough to warrant this. A tub or pillar supported plant should be about three feet tall for placing on the floor.

For climbing plants, a wall bracket is suitable. Many ivies, philodendrons, some peperomias, and several members of the cissus family, such as the Kangaroo vine, go well against a wood-panelled or plain, painted wall common to offices.

Wherever you decide to place your office plant, use as much care in selecting an appropriate container as you would in choosing an accessory for your home.

The wife who presents her husband with a plant for his office might do much to insure its prolonged life and good looks by sending along a note for the secretary with brief instructions about light, watering and dusting. Including a small extra plant for the secretary's own desk would be double insurance of good plant care!

Ivy thrives in bright, moist surroundings, but it is inexpensive to replace if you can't meet these needs.

Fatshedera lizei has big, five-lobed leaves resembling ivy. It is a good upright shrub for a floor plant box.

Dieffenbachias make decorative plants. They are attractive and tolerant of less-than-perfect growing conditions.

Dividing space with greenery

Plants can be more than just decorative. They can be functional, too, grown in a room divider as part of a substitute wall that breaks up a large space.

The modern house, built on an open plan, sometimes includes plant box-dividers as a basic design element. Older homes, too, use dividers to make two rooms out of one large one.

Because they will be prominently displayed, it is doubly important to have only the glossiest, healthiest of plants in your divider. Success can be assured if you choose plants that don't demand sunlight for survival. Aglaonema, syngoniums, philodendrons, and sansevierias, are a few of the foliage plants which grow well in reduced light.

Be careful, if your plant box has no bottom drainage hole, to put in a good layer of pebbles or broken crockery before you put plants in place. Overwatering is a common source of trouble that can be overcome by this step.

Separate space artistically with plants and paintings

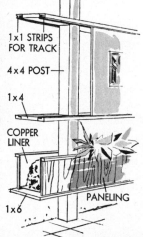

1x1 STRIPS FOR TRACK

4x4 POST

1x4

COPPER LINER

1x6

PANELING

Paintings and plants are good companions for a divider designed to separate the dining and lounge areas of one large room.

The sketch on the left shows construction details, including a copper lining for plant box, with side panelling to match the other woodwork in the room.

The design would be improved if provisions were made to install fluorescent lighting immediately above the plants.

The extra amount of illumination thus supplied would do much to ensure a long and healthy life for plants in a dimly lit situation like this.

Floor-level plant box

If your front door opens directly into the living room, this floor plant box can subtly indicate an entrance area, separate from the rest of the room.

A handyman could easily build one like it to the dimensions you need. Give it a metal liner.

Rubber plant, monstera, sansevieria, philodendron fill it attractively.

A series of open shelves in bookcase style holds a collection of ivies and African violets. If the light is from one side, turn plants regularly so their growth will be even.

The architectural use of plants

Contemporary architecture often sets such a simple background for living that it demands the inclusion of contrasting decorative forms to complete the design.

To make certain that plants will be used and placed to best advantage the architect sometimes builds a plant box into the house, indicating where plants should be placed to complement clean, straight lines.

The sculptured look of big foliage plants is nowhere more striking and appropriate than in such a setting. Leaf patterns against the sweep of a plain wall become much more than a pleasant afterthought.

In such a setting, scale is of foremost importance. Notice that in the room pictured below, anything other than tall, bold-leaved plants would look insignificant.

In the setting across the page, the need for height is reduced, but leaves must be big enough to be seen at a distance before the arrangements can have a proper impact.

Plants reinforce the separation of living-dining areas

Philodendron and dieffenbachia in a brick plant box which is an extension of fireplace wall soften the lines and improve the effect of a room divider.

The plant box on the mantlepiece above lets the philodendron hang downwards gracefully to join the plants at the lower level.

Foliage gives a fresh, inviting air to an entrance hall

Several varieties of philodendron, a palm and two tall rubber plants make interesting patterns against the window and offer both an outdoor and indoor welcome to this home.

Any window, with the exception of those facing south, is a good position for this type of plant. Direct sun does not benefit the plant therefore windows facing east or north are preferable.

◀ A functional use of plants

This modern version of the conservatory brings plants into the living room for use as ornamentation.

Concealed fixtures supply light necessary for plant health and make them look dramatic at the same time.

Philodendron pinnatifidum climbs on tree branches for background height; dieffenbachia takes a centre-front position with dracaena planted at the right and in a floor-level plant box in the hall.

*A cutleaf foliage pattern
brings a good contrast
to a simple interior*

An important plant of monstera in an oriental-type container introduces pattern to the simplicity of a black and white colour scheme where straight lines are a dominant theme.

The exotic look of this plant has made it very popular as an emphasis for contemporary architecture. Its size makes it suitable for use as the one, bold ornament to contrast with its simple background.

A native of tropical America, the monstera is a climbing plant, perfect to grow on a pillar support pole. Enormous leaves (some are over a foot long) are deeply slit and some are pierced with a number of holes along either side of the midrib.

Plants as big as this are in the luxury class, but you can start with young ones and have a large one in time.

This floor plant box is a metal box fronted by a brass fireplace fender. The plants are several varieties of philodendron and dracaena. As for a dish garden, you often get the best effect by including both tall and short plants. Unless the plants receive daylight you must provide daily artificial lighting to keep them alive. A lamp trained on the plants will do this.

Plants to decorate the hall

Your entrance hall should give a warm welcome. This can be done by the presence of foliage plants suitably arranged to do this.

Luxurious tropical plants have an air of opulence that lends easy elegance to a hall or entrance, even though space is limited. Use a massed display or a single plant, depending upon the size of the entrance hall and other furnishings.

Most plants enjoy fresh air, but in cold weather you must be sure that they are not exposed to cold draughts each time the front door is opened. Choose the setting with this in mind.

Use the most attractive containers that you can find, and preserve a polished look by wiping the foliage regularly.

If your hall is without windows, remember to move your plants into sunlight daily if artificial lighting is inadequate.

Foliage creates a flowing line

The leafy grace of large foliage plants on an inset of tile, marble or linoleum makes a nice transition from the entrance to the living room.

Plants with variegated foliage in the foreground are two varieties of dieffenbachia; a large cutleaf monstera is next; at the back, the tallest plants in the group, are scheffleras.

With the plants in pots, you can move them periodically to a brighter place for a light bath; to sink or tub for a shower bath.

Plant stands for a formal hallway ▶

Dark green, heart-shaped leaves of *Philodendron scandens* and its ability to survive in unfavourable light situations make it a favourable foliage plant, deserving of popularity.

As a climbing plant it is well suited to display in plant stands such as these, which are of wrought iron, each holding three pots.

Set clay pots in waterproof containers which will protect the carpet or floor beneath from damage by water. Dust the foliage regularly.

Growing plants for the table

Potted plants make excellent table decorations for special occasions. Like cut flowers, they make even the simplest of meals seem more important.

Colourful flowering plants are an obvious choice for centrepieces. But don't overlook the decorative uses of foliage plants. Arrange them in a vase that will harmonise with the table setting, and you will be surprised at their adaptability.

Pots of ivy, planted in a silver bowl (give it a protective lining of foil) have the look of classic simplicity which is elegant enough for company, but unpretentious enough for the simplest of meals. Make a small dish garden with your favourite foliage plants to brighten your table at mealtimes.

Remember to do the same as you would with flowers and choose low plants that will not interfere with conversation across the table. Wipe or dust each leaf carefully and pinch off any that look faded or unattractive.

Begonias add colour

They are fairly inexpensive to buy and their bloom will last for many weeks if they are moved into the bright sunlight between waterings. These attractive blooms make a colourful display on your table. They require very little attention and the delicate flowers are rewarding. Begonias are favourite potted plants.

Spotlight on clay flowerpots

This is a new idea. Clean small flower pots thoroughly and use them as containers for the sweet. Even without this, a group of small flowering plants in matching pots makes an attractive centrepiece. Stand the pots on concealed coasters or foil discs to protect the cloth.

Potted plants can be disguised to decorate your party table

Azaleas, in a range of whites, pinks and reds, are often a favourite gift. Use your plant to decorate a party table in an attractive fashion.

When the frosts have passed plunge the pot in a shady part of the garden and bring indoors again in autumn.

Foliage and fruit grace your buffet table

Young dieffenbachia and a line of small, inexpensive peperomias (with the cream and green mottlings) back fruit and sweets on a buffet table. Use coasters under the pots.

After peperomias have served their decorative purpose, repot them in larger pots for root growth.

Aluminium plants are stylish

The silvery leaf markings of the inexpensive Aluminium plant (*Pilea cadieri*) make it pretty enough to decorate any table. Wrap pots in paper doilies and put a flowering azalea plant at the back.

Plants look new by candlelight

Candlelight and table accessories are to plants what good clothes are to people. Suddenly, they look brand new; you scarcely recognise them in their fresh attire.

You can't arrange plants as you would cut flowers without damaging them considerably through cutting, but you can combine them with candles and set them in an unusual container to get the effect of an arrangement, just as with fresh flowers.

You can create an original composition by using one of your favourite plants in a new setting. Low-growing ones like African violets, ever-flowering begonias, peperomias, dwarf palms and syngoniums are good for the centre of the table.

Taller ones such as aspidistras, dieffenbachia, rubber plants and dracaenas can all be used on side tables, backed with mirrors, and flanked by candles and other appropriate accessories in decorative designs to suit the occasion.

Red and green makes a cheerful theme for the holiday season

To decorate a festive meal set twin pots of scindapsus at each end of a painted white base or long, narrow tray.

Between the two plants, line up a group of low candles like these, or use the ones you can buy in their own clear glass bowls.

Place your African violet plant in this setting

A hollowed-out piece of driftwood makes a nest for young African violet plants, with strands of moss to disguise the soil they grow in.

Accompanied by two twisted candles in a soft green, they are a good illustration of an ingenious and creative way to use house plants as sophisticated table decorations.

Notice how well the colour is reflected in the table cloth, glasses and china.

◄ A mirror gives twice the effect to a plant arrangment

The maranta, or prayer plant, which gets its name from its habit of folding up its leaves at night, is usually rather colourless and unattractive in appearance.

In this position, however, where it is placed on a sideboard with a mirror behind and matched with a brass candlestick with gleaming red candles it assumes a greater importance and lends interest to what would otherwise be an ordinary situation.

Enhance the natural beauty of plants

Plants displayed with artistic care can be a constant feature in your home. It will take a little time and ingenuity on your part to select vases and accessories in harmony with plants and setting. But you will have added your personal touch to the natural beauty of the plants in a way that is creative, and satisfying.

Do not think you have to go out and buy everything that goes into your arrangement. Take another look at familiar household belongings. A fruit bowl, or metal waste-paper basket may be a handsome accompaniment to plants, and will have the merit of freshness and originality, as a container.

You can experiment with plants by combining them and arranging them in unusual ways. Some are far from spectacular by themselves, but arranged with some other plant they can look quite different. Sansevieria combined with pickaback plant as is shown on the opposite page is an example of an imaginative display.

Use accessories with plants to emphasise a seasonal theme

This is a nice way to express the spirit of Christmas. The grouping of African violets forms a colourful basis for the statue of the Madonna and Child. You can substitute the other plants for the violets.

Accessories, such as figurines, candles and driftwood, can give a finished look to a plant arrangement. They can also help to carry out a holiday seasonal theme.

But do not be too elaborate. If plants are the main feature of your arrangement, use only accessories that emphasise the theme and are in proper scale.

The secret of a good arrangement lies in the careful choice of plants, containers and accessories and organised planning beforehand.

Ivy is complemented
by driftwood

What is more attractive than a curving branch of ivy-entwined driftwood. Help the plant establish itself by securing the tips to the driftwood with some florists' tape or yarn. Pots of marigolds below supply a colour contrast. Ivy looks best when supported by another plant.

Contrasting plants
make a bold, fresh
decoration

Two contrasting plants make an indoor arrangement more exciting and more attractive. Select two that contrast in size, texture, or pattern to complement each other.

Gold-edged sansevieria is never seen to better advantage than when light is shining between its slim, smooth, marble-patterned leaves.

Cross-light also focuses attention on the hairy pickaback plant. Neither require a lot of sun and will thrive on a wall which does not face the light.

To achieve this effect, arrange plants as in the sketch, the tall one at the back, and the shorter one in front. The watertight outer container is filled with pebbles to hide the soil.

Dish gardens

Dish gardens are fun to plant and pretty to look at. They are attractive as table centrepieces or decorations for an end table, buffet or chest.

First, decide where the dish garden is to be displayed. You will plant it differently if it's to be viewed from all sides rather than just from the front.

Select young foliage plants which contrast with each other. Include a variety of height, leaf shape, size, and patterning. Combine plants that have similar light and water needs so all will have a chance to grow.

Your container may be as simple or as elegant as you like, of metal, ceramic or plastic. Your container should not be too shallow. At least three inches of depth is needed for stability and root growing in most plants. Provide drainage with a good bottom layer of pebbles, charcoal, or pieces of broken clay pots.

Display young plants in a mixed plant box

Almost any combination of plants can be grouped into a basic triangle—an aesthetically pleasing shape in a shallow container.

Here the tall plant is aglaonema; the dwarf plant in front is peperomia, with Hahn's sansevieria backing the variegated peperomia (the plant in the centre and right with the most white in its foliage).

Design a long lasting table decoration of foliage

Spear-like sansevieria planted centrally in a low brass dish is nicely contrasted with the heart-shaped leaves of *Philodendron scandens*.

In general, it is most effective to keep the taller plants clumped together, tapering towards the edges of the container with smaller, low-growing plants or climbers like the philodendron.

Planning is important for maximum effect

1 Cover the bottom of the container with a layer of gravel, pebbles, charcoal, or broken clay pots—important since only a few plant boxes have bottom drainage holes. Next, add a layer of potting soil. Buy one of the special potting mixes available at most garden centres, or mix your own by using equal parts of gravel, garden soil, and peat or compost.

Taller plants should be placed at the back of the container

2 Once plants are removed from their pots, try not to disturb the roots more than necessary. Remove soil gently as needed to fit plants into the space. Fill around plants with loose soil only after all are set in place. Then firm the soil with the fingers. Thump container on planting surface once or twice to sift soil around the roots. Water the plant and it will then be ready to be placed on view.

For balance and effect in an arrangement it is important to place taller plants at the back, preferably in a central position.

A light does much to keep the effect of a dish garden

3 The light boost which a near-by table lamp can give a dish garden helps to keep it healthy and growing. All plants used in this one are tolerant of a reduced light situation.

Aglaonema modestum is the tall plant at the centre back; at its left is *Dracaena sanderiana;* to the right *Dracaena godseffiana;* and in front of it, *Peperomia obtusifolia variegata.* The vine is *Scindapsus aureus.*

CHAPTER 2

Favourite foliage plants

Green is a colour you never tire of as it is always pleasing to the eye and fits well with any room. That is one reason why foliage plants are such perennial favourites. Indoors, in winter, their green leaves hint at the summer to come; in summertime, they look cool and refreshing when temperatures rise.

Another reason why everyone likes foliage plants is because they have a good appearance all the year round. Foliage plants are never out of season but you can still appreciate them in the same way as you do seasonal flowering plants.

You cannot possibly grow all the foliage plants you may wish. So use the pictures and information on the following pages to select those with the qualities you most admire, and which are best suited to the growing conditions in your home.

All of these foliage plants will thrive in any living room

1. Kentia palm is graceful, hardy, and suited to home growing conditions.
2. Philodendron with reddish underleaf.
3. Fiddleleaf fig leaves look like green polished leather. Makes a tree.
4. Philodendron with scalloped leaf edge.
5. *Dieffenbachia picta superba* foliage is a deep green usually splashed with white.
6. Aralia leaf outline is like a starburst.
7. Monstera, called Gruyère cheese plant.
8. Kangaroo vine is a pretty trailer.

Large, attractive plants

The luxury look comes easily and quickly to your rooms when you invest in suitable plants of larger size. If time is not important, you can start with young plants and enjoy them as they grow.

Big plants require some space around them, and also large containers so that they will have a well-balanced, stable appearance. They need little attention and extensive daily care is not essential.

Rubber plant, fiddleleaf fig, and birdsnest fern on the opposite page, and schefflera below all like a filtered or reflected light, but not direct sun. The fern, especially, looks best placed below eye-level, so you can see into its rosette-shaped crown. All these plants can be suitably placed on the floor or near a wall or window.

◄ Large glossy leaves are common to this trio

Ficus elastica decora (or doe-scheri) thrives at a temperature of 65° in a good light. It grows slowly and seldom requires shifting to a larger pot.

Fiddleleaf fig (Ficus lyrata) has the same growing needs as the rubber plant. Watch both for leaf drop due to poor light and too much water.

Birdsnest fern (Asplenium nidus) likes a moist soil, rich in organic materials and peat moss or leaf mould.

A popular newcomer

Schefflera is not a new plant, though its popularity is fairly recent. It is fashionable and very decorative for planting in the hall.

It has a good green colour, rounded outlines and the leaves are grouped. It needs good light but not direct sun and it grows somewhat faster than the fig or rubber tree. Overwatering will cause the bottom leaves to drop.

Coloured foliage plants are exotic

Green is as basic a colour among growing plants indoors as it is in the garden, but just as outdoors one looks also for colour in foliage as well as in flowers, so many of the plants suitable for our homes provide us with colourful leaves. All the tints, tones and shades of the rainbow can be brought into the home if one chooses with care.

Remember that as a general rule plants with coloured foliage require more light than those with plain green leaves. But direct sunlight is only for the cacti and succulents; some leaves may burn and show brown spots.

Many normally greenhouse plants, particularly from the ivy and fig (ficus) family, are available in variegated form, splashed, streaked or mottled with gold, cream or white. Some other plants are still more vivid, containing scarlet, purple, magenta, pink, orange and silver in their leaves. Look to the begonias, particularly the rex varieties for vivid colour and interesting texture. Grow the geraniums for their leaves as well as their flowers. Dracaenas, cordylines, neoregelias all have burning colours in their foliage. The striped zebra plant or aphelandra is attractive for its bright leaves as well as its brilliant cockscomb of flower.

This flowering plant is grown for its foliage

Geraniums are deservedly popular. They are easy to grow and to propagate. They flourish indoors and out during the summer months and give lavishly of their vivid flowers. Many, however, have colourful foliage too. Pelargonium Happy Thought, shown here, is also known as the Butterfly geranium because of the mark in the centre of each leaf. It also produces crimson flowers.

The croton plant is noted for its different coloured leaves

Croton plants are not expensive to buy, but they are difficult to grow at home because they need stronger light and higher humidity than can readily be supplied indoors.

Even though they are not long-lasting house plants, you will enjoy having one around if you regard it as you would cut flowers, which are discarded when withered.

Coleus is an easily cultivated plant

Coleus plants can be kept young, short and fresh by rooting their tips in soil or water when the stems become too tall.

If the plant receives sufficient sunlight the colours are brilliant. If you are displaying it in dim light, it should be moved to a sunny window regularly.

A favourite parlour plant

Saxifraga sarmentosa is this plant's botanical name. It is also called a strawberry-begonia and strawberry-geranium, although strawberry saxifrage is a more accurate label.

The 'strawberry' part of its name comes from its interesting habit of putting out aerial runners, like a garden strawberry, which bear new plantlets at their ends.

New variety shown here is rare, but still lovely older varieties have foliage that is grey-green above and purple below. They all like moist soil and medium light. All varieties are the easiest of plants to propagate.

For directions on how to have more, see the section on reproduction by runners in the final chapter.

Begonias are among the most

beautiful of foliage plants

Begonias which are among the most popular of house plants are grown more for their foliage than their flowers. Their leaves stay attractive all year long, and if you give them adequate light and water some will bloom in winter.

Major classifications of begonias

Tuberous begonias are discussed elsewhere, as are the fibrous-root varieties known as 'everblooming'. Most of those shown here are of the semituberous and rhizomatous types, having a creeping stem and leaves with long hairs. In the Rex group you find purplish leaf backgrounds with silvery surface. Beefsteak begonias (*B. feasti*) have deep red undersides that contrast with the smooth, shiny, green tops of their leaves.

Begonias are easily grown

They appreciate humid air and in warm rooms like a soil that is constantly moist but not wet. The least hint of gas in the atmosphere will kill them.

In winter, they need all the sunlight you can give them: indirect but bright light is best for the rest of the year. Foliage becomes pale when the sun is too bright. Begonias will tolerate temperature variations, but thrive between 65 and 70 degrees.

When potting, set each plant with its crown barely above the soil but not in a depression where water can collect next to the stems. Soil should be light and porous, slightly acid, and contain some peat moss.

◀ *Three choices from the large range of begonias*

The Rex begonia at the left deserves a special mention since its hybrids now number in the hundreds and are among the loveliest of house plants.

Its heart-shaped leaves are marked, zoned, or spotted with silver, rose and green.

The smooth-leaved *B. sanguinea* next to it has underleaves the colour of red leather. *B. maculata* displays silver specks on its foliage. The last chapter tells how to multiply any of the plants shown here by means of a leaf cutting.

Leaf types

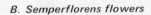

B. Semperflorens flowers

B. Semperflorens

B. glabra

B. luxurians

B. heracleifolia

B. lucerna

B. fuchsioides rosea

B. ricinifolia

B. dregei

B. feasti

B. rex

B. haageana

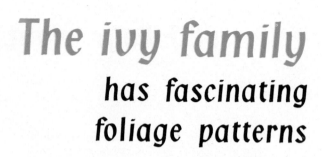

The ivy family
has fascinating foliage patterns

Some of the easiest, most accommodating, most versatile and varied of our house plants are to be found in the ivy or hedera family. They are climbers which can grow to the ceiling or cover a wall, will trail prettily from a wall mounting or will form a low growing mass of foliage. Colours can be various tints and shades of green, or green with white, grey, cream, yellow and gold. Ivies grow wild in this country which indicates to us that they are easy to grow indoors.

The botanical name for ivy is *Hedera helix*, the 'Hedera' being latin for ivy and 'helix' meaning a snail, thus describing the twisting and twining habit of the plant. Ivy is, in fact, one of our few evergreen climbing plants which grows and attaches itself to trees and walls by a series of aerial roots. There are a number of forms of both wild ivy and cultivated varieties for the garden.

Indoor ivies are, of course, derived basically from wild ivy, Hedera helix, but hybridisers have produced many finer forms which are daintier, prettier, have a more leafy habit and a greater colour range. On some indoor ivies it is possible to see aerial roots growing on the stems as very coarse, short hairs, but mainly because of the lack of indoor humidity these roots are too weak and ineffective to play any part. So to grow a climbing ivy indoors it is necessary to give it support in the form of a cane or a mossed stick to which it must be trained

Hedera helix Chicago

Top Left   Hedera helix Chicago
The Americans find ivy difficult to grow and have produced many hybrids to suit their conditions. This is one of the best.

Hedera helix cristata

Bottom Left   Hedera helix cristata.
The crinkled edges of the leaves make this plant unusual among ivies and have given it the popular name of Holly Ivy.

Hedera helix sagittifolia

Right   Hedera sagittifolia
Thin, arrow-head leaves are produced in great profusion by this variety, which looks better as a trailer than a climber.

Ivies like plenty of water during summer when they are growing well but should be kept just moist in winter. A light feed during the warmer months will keep plants growing well and aid the production of fresh growth. Plain green varieties require rather less light than variegated kinds, but none should have direct sunlight for long periods.

Plants are comparatively easy to propagate. Shoots a few inches in length will frequently put out roots if the end is placed in a cup or phial of water alone. In some conditions a shoot pressed into the soil of the pot will begin to grow. The most foolproof method of growing a new plant, however, is by layering.

A growing shoot from the plant is slightly cracked or cut and pinned (a hairpin will do) to the soil of the same or another pot nearby. Roots are formed at this point and after a few weeks the shoot joining the new plant can be cut.

New ivy hybrids are constantly appearing under a number of names. Differences between some of these new varieties and some of the old are sometimes difficult to detect and usually amount to better colour, better leaf shape, greater leaf formation or hardier, tougher habit.

All the varieties listed on this page are comparatively modern and easily obtained. All will grow well in the average home.

Hedera helix glacier

Top Right   Hedera helix glacier
A pretty little ivy with leaves mainly white edged and blotched with grey-green. Glacier is a rewarding plant to grow.

Hedera marmorata

Bottom Right   Hedera marmorata
With marbled and flecked leaves in cream, gold and white, marmorata has large leaves growing in abundance.

Emerald Gem has
leaves like arrowheads

Syngonium podophyllum, the botanical name for the plant of which this creeper is a cultivated variety, is easy to grow. It likes ordinary house temperatures, 60-70°, and can tolerate low light. Eventually, it becomes stringy-looking if grown too long in a dark spot.

Give these plants well-drained soil rich in organic matter; or use peat alone to get good results. A moist soil is preferred, but these plants are inclined to become soft if they are overwatered.

White-veined Fittonia
requires light and humidity

Fittonia is not a strong plant but it is very attractive. Its main beauty lies in the lacy veining on its leaves. Its botanical name is *Fittonia argyroneura.* Another member of the family, which is equally attractive is the red-veined *Fittonia verschaffeltii* that has the same kind of cultural needs.

To provide the humid air that is necessary, keep a clear plastic cake cover over the plant most of the time or grow it in a terrarium.

Four climbing
and trailing plants

To display climbing and trailing plants to best advantage, place them in a setting where they are allowed to follow their natural growth patterns. On tables, window ledges, shelves and in plant boxes, they can trail gracefully over the edge, following their natural inclinations.

The syngoniums (Emerald Gem, shown here, is but one of a big plant group) are well adapted to a moss stick planting. The pickaback plant makes a suitable partner for the more upright plants in a dish garden.

For an indoor display where you want background greenery, train a kangaroo vine to climb a trellis.

A wicker basket can serve as a plant container

One of the few house plants which comes from North America, the Pickaback plant (*Tolmeia menziesii*) ranks amongst the hardier trailers.

A major attraction is its curious habit of putting out new plants at the base of old leaves—thus its popular name.

To obtain additional plants peg the young plant to the soil in a small pot placed nearby until it roots; cut free and you have a new plant.

The Pickaback plant grows best in bright light or sun, and in a uniformly moist soil.

BREADBASKET

SAUCER

Kangaroo vine is easily grown

Kangaroo vine gets its common name from Australia and its botanical name *Cissus antarctica* indicates that it comes from the southern hemisphere. It is similar to, and frequently confused with, the Grape Ivy, or *Rhoicissus rhomboidea*.

It requires a light, well-drained soil and does best in filtered sunlight. Do not over-water or allow the surface soil to become dry before adding water. It prefers a room temperature of 55-65°.

It is readily propagated from cuttings, and is one of the most satisfactory vines for indoor use. It looks well in an indoor plant box or in a dish garden.

Vines that complement each other

In a wall container, try a combination of vines that add to each other's looks. Here, Canary Ivy; with variegated foliage, looks better for the addition of philodendron.

Place climbing plants for maximum effect

Climbing plants can hold their own with the most aristocratic of house plants if they have the right setting and container.

They are always useful in combination with bigger or upright-growing specimens in an indoor plant-box. Vines need not always take a back seat. Use a little imagination in the way you display them, and vines alone can do an impressive job of decoration.

Ivy is suitable

for a masculine setting

Any one of many ivy varieties would be suitable for combining with a wooden decoy and handsome pewter plate, shown against a wood-panelled wall. To keep the ivy growing luxuriantly, you must supply bright light and adequate moisture. Placing the ivy on a shelf makes the most of its natural growth and gives it an edge over which to trail its curving stems, creating a naturalistic effect.

A new look for a well known philodendron

Because it is so easily and so widely grown, this philodendron is sometimes taken for granted as a house plant.

But give it a polished brass mortar and pestle set as a container, and you could not wish for a more elegant climber.

Philodendron, like all others, thrives in a moist soil and with-stands a low light situation, but grows more luxuriantly in medium light. It will grow in water, but its leaves may become too widely spaced.

The colourful leaf pattern of variegated Canary Ivy is well suited to growing on a moss stick

This is a dramatic way to display a climber. The creamy-white leaf markings of a variegated Canary ivy plant display to maximum advantage against a plain background. The design of the ceramic jardinière makes its contribution to the effect.

This is not an easily grown house plant, but it does repay you for extra effort with its elegant appearance.

Hedera canariensis folius variegatus needs a brightly lit or sunny location if it is to grow well.

It also demands more humidity than is ordinarily available indoors in wintertime. You can supplement humidity by keeping the moss stick on which it is growing constantly moist, and by spraying the foliage frequently with tepid water. It is wise to do this over a sink.

The decorative monsteras and philodendrons

*The increasing assortment
of philodendrons offers
beautiful and durable foliage*

The collection of philodendrons pictured on the left is but a sample of the variety of leaf shapes and sizes included in the philodendron family.

Shown with them is their close ally, *Monstera deliciosa,* often sold as cutleaf philodendron, and called a Swiss Cheese or Gruyère plant because of the holes that perforate the large split leaves next to the central rib. Monstera has much the same needs as the philodendrons.

Natives of the tropical jungles of Central and South America, the philodendrons have become the most popular of indoor foliage plants.

*Monstera is a favourite
of decorators because of
its sophisticated appearance*

For modern interiors that depend on solid colours and the sweep of plain, undecorated surfaces to achieve major effects, the big, deeply split leaves of monstera can often add the proper amount of contrasting pattern.

The several varieties of monstera require somewhat brighter light than philodendrons and a larger container or the leaves will not split to the extent that they should.

In all other requirements, monstera is like the philodendrons and needs a loose, porous soil; sufficient water to keep soil moist, not wet; and average temperatures of from 60-70°

Philodendrons make a good combination in a dish garden

Young monstera plants often have leaves that are entire or show only a few splits. As the plant grows older, if given a large pot and the right light and moisture, it puts out larger leaves which are much more profusely slit.

This philodendron (*scandens*) also varies greatly in the size and spacing of its foliage depending on the conditions under which it is grown.

If grown over a period of time in poor light and low humidity, this vine becomes stringy, puny, and new leaves become smaller and smaller. To start a new vine, take a sturdy tip cutting which you must then root.

These three varieties require little attention

Philodendron varieties shown, left to right are: *P. bipinnatifidum, P. fenzlii, P. erubescens.*

Of the three, fenzlii is probably best suited to growing on a moss stick, since it has the strongest climbing tendency. It is also called a fiddle-leaf philodendron and grows more rapidly than the larger leaved varieties.

Philodendron bipinnatifidum, is one of the most reliable of the fern-like varieties. Others which resemble it are *P. laciniosum, P. selloum,* and *P. elegans* which are all deeply lobed.

Other philodendrons having a shield-shaped leaf, something like *erubescens* include: *P. cordatum,* like a larger *scandens, P. imbe,* large again, the similar, but more practically sized *P. sagettifolium;* and the attractive, silver spotted *P. sodiroi.*

Make your own moss sticks

A moss stick

cylinder for

growing your

favourite climber

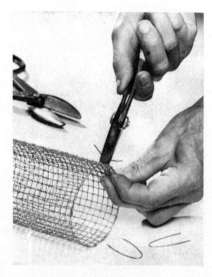

Gold-splashed scindapsus is the vine used for this display. It requires humidity and bright light to thrive. For a dimly lit spot, try philodendron instead.

1 The basic cylinder is made of $\frac{1}{4}$ inch square plastic mesh. Buy a 10 inch strip, either 30 or 36 inches wide, depending on how tall you want the arrangement to be when finished.

Roll the mesh into a cylinder. Overlap edges about $\frac{3}{4}$ of an inch and fasten it at 6 inch intervals with strands of wire. Cut off the surplus wire

2 Put an inch or two of gravel in the tub for drainage. Push two small sticks through the bottom of the cylinder to help brace it. Flat sticks are best and can be slipped in if the mesh is cut slightly. Use standard potting soil mixture to fill the tub.

3 Make a mixture of half peat or shredded moss, and half vermiculite or perlite. To damp the mixture properly, soak peat or moss overnight.

A paper funnel is a help in filling. Stop at intervals as you fill and tamp mixture down with broom handle.

4 Space vines around the pole in tub, use 3 to 5 for an arrangement of this size. Use any favourite vine. Cover the roots with soil to within an inch of the rim to allow room for watering. Vines planted in this way will soon give you an effective display.

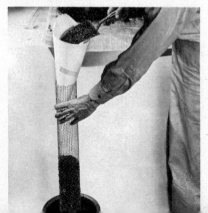

Care after planting

Train by twisting vines to grow in a spiral around the pole. Pin the vines to the pole with hairpins inserted at a sharp angle.

Push a small pot into the cylinder top. Fill it with water which will seep down into the pole and provide moisture in which support roots can grow. Add water daily.

When you water, fill the tub to the brim and let the water settle. Continue watering until it drains out at the bottom. Let the surface dry before re-watering.

Another kind of moss stick

Choose a stake no longer than 2 feet. Spread a pound of dampened sphagnum moss on paper, as shown. To start, roll the edge of the paper with the moss for a half-turn. Press firm as you roll.

Use rustproof wire
to hold sphagnum moss
on a wooden plant stake

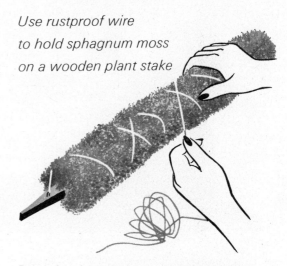

Fasten the wire at the bottom of the stake; wind spiral upwards, with turns about 2 inches apart. Adjust the moss to cover the top of the stake and spiral down to the base and fasten. If the moss stick looks ragged, wrap it tightly in paper for 15 minutes.

Insert the moss stick firmly in the pot. Plant the vines at its base. To help them establish themselves, fasten the tips to the moss stick with hairpins or staples.

For success with an arrangement of this type, the moss stick must be kept constantly moist.

Striking foliage

If your home is small and space for plants limited, this group will interest you.

None of the plants shown grows large under average home conditions, though syngonium (left) can be trained to climb a moss stick. All have intriguing foliage that is remarkable for pattern or for shape.

◄ Divided leaves of a rich, dark green

Syngonium auritum or 'Five Fingers', is the name given to this dainty climber. It is grown in a pot, and resembles the Goosefoot plant, also a syngonium pictured opposite. Young plants are upright, climbing as they mature.

There is a large choice
of small peperomias

All peperomias like medium light and warm temperatures, not below 60 degrees at night. Grow them in porous soil and do not overwater.

Varieties pictured are *P. caperata* at each end of plant box; *P. magnoliaefolia,* showing a good deal of white in its foliage; a trailing type *P. glabella* in front; solid green *P. obtusifolia* in the rear; and *P. argyreia,* or Watermelon peperomia, with silvery leaf markings.

patterns make these plants worth a second look

These plants—some common, some rare—will grow slowly, without taking too much room

Goosefoot plant has cream-tinted foliage

The Goosefoot Plant, *Syngonium podophyllum,* also *lineatum,* is an easily grown plant that will tolerate low light. Grow it in a loose loam or peat moss.

Aphelandra has a patent-leather gloss

This distinctive plant needs sun and high humidity if it is to thrive. Its most popular form is usually sold with a bright yellow cockscomb of flower at the top.

Star-shape marks Norfolk Island Pine

Grow it in sunlight and syringe needle-like foliage frequently as a means of increasing the humidity. Botanically, it is an *Araucaria excelsa.*

A marbled mass of foliage

The shape, colour and habit of *Dracaena godseffiana florida* are quite different from those of most other dracaenas. Blotched and speckled leaves are green and white.

Painted fingernail plant turns scarlet

When the insignificant flowers appear in the centre of *Nidularium marechati,* the centre of the leaves turn a vivid scarlet from their normal dark green.

Dracaena

Trio of dracaenas in a corner grouping

The largest plant (rear) is *Dracaena fragrans massangeana*, also called the Corn Plant. In the foreground are two specimens of *D. deremensis* which are sharply striped with white and grey. Once established these plants will live for a long time.

Smaller varieties make good centrepieces

Dracaena godseffiana is quite unlike the other members of its family in appearance, having yellow-dotted, glossy green leaves on wiry stems. Little *D. sanderi* has two white bands bordering a grey-green central stripe.

Common striped dracaena has so often been relegated to the background of a large indoor display that it acquires a fresh and unusual air when brought out of its corner and shown as an independent plant.

Smaller dracaenas, too, have enough character to warrant their more frequent use as single plants, as they are attractive in their own right. *D. godseffiana* and *D. sanderi*, both of which are pictured below, are among the best of the dwarf-growing types.

Regardless of size, dracaenas in general thrive on damp soil, prividing drainage is good and temperatures fairly high, not dropping below 55° at night. Dracaenas do well either in bright or in medium light.

If the leaf tips become brown, it is usually a sign of improper watering. Too little or too much watering will produce that condition.

Treat it properly and dracaena is ▶
suited to any setting

One of the commonest varieties of dracaena, *Dracaena fragrans massangeana*, will win enthusiastic praise if you dress it with an attractive cover, and place it where it can be admired from all sides. Do take precautions against water marks (see sketch and suggestions below), or set pot into a glazed ceramic jardinière. Closely related to the dracaenas, and sometimes sold under this name, are the cordylines, generally similar in shape, and sometimes red and purple in colour.

ELASTIC POT COVER OF STRAW

POT

ALUMINUM FOIL TO PREVENT LEAKAGE

WOOD BLOCK

is a versatile plant that merits attention

A number of interesting species have leaves that are long and broad, striped in white or yellow

Palms *give an air of elegance*

Palms and elegance go well together. When informality was the dominant decorative style, potted palms were out of fashion. Now that a return to elegance is a noticeable decorating trend, palms are in vogue.

Of the palms small enough to be suitable for growing indoors, the most popular are *Howea belmoreana* (Kentia), the miniature date palm from India, *Phoenix roebeleni*, and the slender *Neanthe elegans*.

An undemanding house plant

Palms grow so slowly indoors that they may be kept in the same pot for years by unpotting and removing about a quarter of the root system each year. They prefer a container that seems small in proportion to their over-all size and height.

This means water requirements must be checked frequently. Palms should not dry out completely. If this happens, plunge the pot in water and leave until the soil is saturated.

Use palms as a centrepiece

Sold under various trade names, young palm plants are often used in dish gardens. Try planting three in a sophisticated container to use as a long-lasting table decoration.

In a container like this, put in a layer of pebbles first to supply bottom drainage.

Kentia palm suits an
ultra-modern interior

A Kentia palm in an outer container of gleaming brass adds a refreshing touch of greenery in an otherwise functionally decorated room. The brass container is also useful for protecting the floor from water stains.

One of the favourite indoor palms

The bamboo palm (*Chamaedorea erumpens*) is a slender palm that grows tall without being very wide or spreading. It tolerates dry air, but needs moist soil.

A miniature indoors

The *Phoenix dactylifera* is the date palm and outdoors in its native lands it grows to 100 ft. Home conditions keep it to a more reasonable size. It likes warmth, plenty of light and a well-drained soil that is kept constantly moist though not wet.

Ferns require some shade and a rich loam

◄ *Place ferns where nothing will rub against delicate fronds*

Birdsnest Fern (*Asplenium nidus*), native of Brazil, puts out a whorl of spatula-shaped fronds which grow to two feet or more in length. It is most attractive as a house plant when it is young.

To thrive, ferns need filtered sunlight. Grow them in soil that is rich in organic matter—50 per cent or more of peat. A moist but well-drained soil is best.

You will like the long appearance of Pteris major ►

Pteris major is a relative of the trembling fern (*P. tremula*). Like all other ferns it likes a damp atmosphere and humidity. They require a lot of water in spring and a minimum of water in winter.

When a fern becomes potbound remove it from the pot, separate the roots making two or more plants.

◄ *An old-fashioned looking fern that has returned to popularity*

Whitman, Curly, Crested, Ostrich-plume—these are some of the names by which the more finely divided varieties of the common Boston Fern are known.

As natives of tropical regions, ferns dislike cold. They grow best at a minimum temperature of 55 degrees. In winter sit ferns back from windows so that frond ends do not touch the cold glass.

No special care is required by these plants

A less exacting group of plants than the collection shown here would be hard to find. They can withstand almost any indoor adversity except overwatering.

Except for the screwpine, which does need some filtered sunlight, they have the ability to survive in quite dim corners.

Give these plants a porous soil, adequate drainage, water them sparingly and they will live for years. For appearances sake, dust them occasionally with a dampened cloth so that their somewhat leathery foliage will be at its polished, glossy best.

Aspidistra will grow anywhere

For durability under the least favourable of conditions, the aspidistra or cast-iron plant is hard to equal. It grows best in a shaded spot.

Members of the succulent family, the sansevierias need very little water

The tall variety is *S. zeylanica;* the rosette is a new sport of the familiar dark green *S. hahnii.* This one is called Golden Hahnii after the two gold bands that run the length of each leaf. Use sansevierias in plant boxes and dish gardens, but do not combine them with plants which need large amounts of water.

Striped Bowstring Hemp is a favourite

Its botanical name is *S. trifasciata laurentii*. Planted with heartleaf philodendron, it grows well in low light. It makes a good choice for either the home or office.

The rubber plant grows to tree size

Variegated Indian rubber plant. *Ficus elastica variegata*, makes a handsome room decoration. It can withstand neglect and lack of sunlight, but do not overwater.

A dignified Sansevieria

Sansevieria hahnii is the original variety, quieter and more dignified than the golden type. Its leaves are dark green mottled with grey.

Sword-like leaves have spiny margins

Pandanus or screwpine thrives in warm indoor temperatures. Water moderately in summer but keep definitely on dry side in winter. It needs filtered sunlight.

Dieffenbachias
flourish in filtered light

Dieffenbachias are big, luxuriant plants that catch and hold attention in any room setting which allows them space to spread out their decorative foliage.

There are some 20 varieties of the plant in cultivation, most having dark green foliage with creamy white or pale chartreuse markings or variegations.

A common name for the plant (botanically called after the German physician and botanist J. F. Dieffenbach) is Dumb Cane. It is so called because those who chew it temporarily lose the power of speech. Under no circumstances should any portion of the plant be placed in the mouth.

The dieffenbachia grows best in a well-drained soil rich in organic matter: half garden loam, half peat would be a good mixture. Although it will stay alive and grow slowly in very dim corners, it needs some filtered light if it is to prosper.

When grown in poor light, the plant's natural tendency to become 'leggy' is greatly increased. When the bare stem becomes too long, use the process of air layering, explained in the final chapter, to re-root the plant.

◀ *This variety is generously splashed with chartreuse*

The variety *D. picta roehrsii* with its markings of chartreuse green, makes a bright addition to your colour scheme.

As for all dieffenbachias, keep the soil in which it is growing uniformly moist, but not wet.

Grow it either as a single specimen or in combination with other plants in an indoor planter.

Some varieties have white feathering on green foliage ▶

All dieffenbachia varieties known as picta (which means 'painted') show varying amounts of white patterning or veining.

Two of those recommended are *D. picta memoria* and *D. picta bausei. Dieffenbachia amoena* also displays white markings, but it is so large a plant that it should be used only where there is ample space for growth.

Bromeliads are worth growing for their exotic blooms and ornamental foliage

A delightfully bizarre group of plants, the bromeliads have long been displayed in botanical garden exhibits, attracting attention with their brilliant blooms and neat rosettes of foliage, often so shiny as to appear varnished.

Many can really be classed as succulents since they often store an emergency supply of water, not inside fleshy leaves as succulents do, but within a natural vase-shaped centre formed by their durable foliage.

Natives of the tropical forests of Central and South America, bromeliads fall into two distinct groups: terrestrials, which grow in soil or between rocks; epiphytes, which are tree-dwellers. In the second group, many can exist for long periods without roots, as long as they receive moisture from the reservoirs located in their leaf bases.

In spite of their exotic looks and growth habits, many bromeliads are easy to grow. The main requirement is that the growing medium (osmunda fern root fibre is recommended) be kept moist; the cups at the leaf bases should be filled at each watering.

In winter showy spikes of bloom appear which may remain attractive for several months

Variesia carinata, on the left, is one of the best bromeliads for decorative use because of its feathered crimson and yellow bracts and pale green foliage.

Aechmea fulgens, centre, from Brazil produces spikes tipped with violet flowers; the red berries illustrated here appear later.

Purple-flowered *Tillandsia lindeniana,* although scarcely recognised as such, is a close relative of the Spanish Moss which drapes itself on trees throughout the Deep South of America. From Peru, this is one of the rarer bromeliads.

Almost the only house-plant pest to attack the bromeliads is leaf scale. Usually it can be successfully cured by sponging foliage with warm, soapy water and rinsing with warm clear water.

They are members of the pineapple family

On the left, the somewhat rare *Aechmea macra-cantha* has the wine-red foliage; centre plant is of the cryptanthus species; on the right is *Cryptanthus fosterianus*. These bromeliads grow best in filtered sunlight.

Tree-dwelling bromeliads set on a curving wooden branch imitate the natural habitat

To emphasise the spectacular character of these odd plants; grow them on a bromeliad tree.

Wash the soil gently from the roots and wrap them in pre-dampened osmunda fibre. Use fine wire to secure moss about the roots and to fasten the plant to the tree branch.

When watering, use a spray bulb to moisten the moss and remember to fill the natural cups at the leaf bases with water.

Growing in the large pot at the base of the bromeliad tree is *Vriesia splendens*, perched just above it is a vriesia hybrid and at the top of the branch is *Tillandsia lindeniana*. The smaller pot contains a cryptanthus hybrid. Rotting off at the base is one of the hazards of pot-grown bromeliads. This is caused by excessive moisture and can be avoided by supplying a good bottom drainage.

Most varieties of this type of bromeliad

have foliage mottled with red or maroon

A neoregelia hybrid with its rich mottled colouring makes an eye-catching display in any setting. The blooms are fiery-red and bell-shaped. *Neoregelia spectabilis,* a popular variety of this bromeliad, has metallic green leaves which end in pronounced tips of contrasting blood reds. This accounts for its common name of the Painted Fingernail plant.

The variety of bromeliads attracts collectors

Bromeliads are plants greatly favoured by the collector because they have such a wide range of colour and design. Some varieties of this rosette-shaped family have exotically coloured leaves while others have subtle shade contrasts in the form of faint bands of colour running the length of the leaf.

They are easy to grow and maintain and although they will live in dim light, they need filtered sunlight if they are to flower indoors. An occasional feeding with organic fertiliser is beneficial.

Three varieties of bromeliads ▶

that will lift your spirits

Vriesia fenestralis (left) has a distinctive dense whorl of broad foliage decorated with a network of fine darker green lines.

Accompanying it are an unusual nidularium, its lettuce-green leaves striped with ivory; and (foreground) another member of the vriesia group.

Pebble mulch used in the pots is attractive and is also practical since it helps to lessen the evaporation from the porous growing fibre.

◀ *Unexpected colourings and forms*

have the appearance of man-made art

Billbergias, of which this is an example, are among the most frequently encountered and fastest growing of the bromeliads.

The easiest method of propagation is by means of division. The small offshoot at the left of the parent plant can be removed and potted separately. It will produce its own bloom by the following year.

Cactus plants belong to the big succulent family

All cactus plants are succulents, though the reverse is not true. There are nearly 30 separate groups of plants that include varieties which are succulents, the cactus being but one of the tribe. And since it is not always easy to be certain which of the thorny and prickly plants is a true cactus, it is safest to refer to all plants in the group with the general term 'succulents.'

Succulence in a plant means the ability to store water. Among the succulents are some of the most highly varied and remarkably well adapted plants in the world—able to exist on high mountains, in deserts, on the seashore, and in tropical jungles.

This genius for survival in unfavourable settings is due to their cell structure, as shown in the diagram opposite. Success with succulents will be more assured once you understand their composition, and their special requirements concerning heat, light, soil and water.

Succulents are 90 per cent water. Enlarged cross section of stem

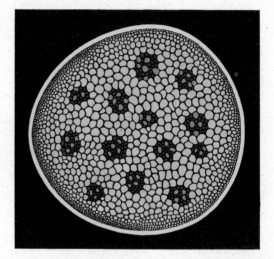

A slightly waxy outer skin, almost impervious to water and gases, the leaves and stems.

Small, hard-walled cells inside the skin are a barrier to escape of water from the big, thin-walled cells which are the inner reservoirs for food and water.

Scattered throughout the mass of inner cells are water tubes, several in a group. They conduct the water taken in by the roots up through the plant.

Specialized tubes carrying food run alongside water tubes but conduct in both directions, letting the succulents live on reserves between rains.

Dish garden of cactus and succulents ▶

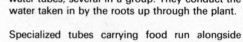

Identify plants by the numbered drawing at left. The succulents are; (1) *Haworthia fasciata*; (4) *Sedum adolphi*; (6) *Stapelia nobilis*. True cactus: (2) *Mammillaria kewensis*; (3) *Trichocereus spachianus*; and (5) *Opuntia leucotricha*.

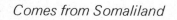

Comes from Somaliland

Kalanchoe somaliensis has attractive glossy leaves, with sawtoothed margins. The mature plant is about 1 foot tall.

*Euphorbia pedilanthus
tithymaloides*

Echeveria secundia   *Sedum pachyphyllum*   *Sedum adolphi*

Jadeplant has a tree-like shape

Crassula argentea (botanical name of this popular succulent) branches, and grows old beautifully. This one's over a foot tall; some grow to 3 feet or taller as potted plants.

A succulent dish garden is exotic

Crassula arborescens is tall plant at back; leaning out at right is *Crassula perforata* (String o' Buttons) *Sedum adolphi* and echeveria are low, rosette shapes in front.

Plants that look like works of art

Succulent plants take so many fascinating shapes and forms, and so many of them have dwarf or small growth patterns that they make ideal house plants. Their sculptured looks are suited to unusual containers. Shallow bowls and dishes make good sites for desert scenes featuring an assortment of your favourites.

These plants are easy to grow—providing you can give succulents good sun and the right amount of water. Resist the temptation to overwater, for this will quickly produce rot. Wait, until the soil is dry to the touch, then water thoroughly, ensuring an adequate bottom drainage.

Equal parts of coarse sand or gravel and garden loam make a good soil—porous enough to drain excess water, yet firm enough to hold the required amount of moisture. Succulents need more water during periods of rapid growth (in summer) and less during the winter when plants are in their dormant season.

◀ Succulents belong to many different plant families

Euphorbias also called 'Devil's spine'. Bryophyllum produces young plants on the leaf edges; Echeveria sends up a circle of young plants around the mother plant; *Sedum pachyphyllum* leaves turn red in the sun *Sedum adolphi* foliage has a powdery, grey-green colour.

Bryophyllum pinnatum

So bizarre and intriguing are succulents that collectors of this family never seem to find all the species they desire. But it is easy to grow more to trade with fellow collectors.

Spring and summer are best for taking cuttings, since plants are in their growing phase and success is most assured.

Many succulents grow offsets at soil level. Detach the offset from its mother plant and insert it in soil which is half coarse sand and half garden loam. Keep dry a few days and then water as usual.

Make stem and leaf cuttings

Danger of rot is greater for stem or leaf cuttings than for offsets. Guard against it by allowing the cutting to dry off for a few days in a cool, shaded spot.

When the wound has 'healed over,' plant the cutting in damp—not wet—sand. Leave it there, watering sparingly until it has taken root before transplanting to the usual sand and loam mixture. Cuttings handled this way should root in a few weeks.

Combine contrasting varieties

Here are two curious succulents to silhouette against a plain wall: metallic-coloured rosettes of echeverias, and the lanky euphorbias which discourage familiarities by means of their armour of make-believe thorns.

Place a dish garden outdoors

Both crassulas and echeverias grow in the rosette shapes which predominate in this succulent dish garden. The tall blooms at the back are of the kalanchoe. Plants that look like clusters of beads are of the sedum group.

Among the best of aloes

Aloe arborescens is well known for its statuesque lines. In its native habitat, it grows to a height of 15 feet. It produces red flowers at the end of winter.

endless variety of shapes and sizes

Strong leaf patterns give this variety its common name of partridge breast

Another much-sought-after succulent is this *Aloe variegata*. It grows in rosettes which are triangular in shape, its leaves edged and marbled sharply with white on dark green.

If succulents interest you, the aloes are worth getting to know. Botanists have identified more than 200 varieties ranging in size from 3 or 4 inches to trees of 30 to 40 feet in height.

Fascinating foliage makes this kalanchoe a good potted plant

Brown-pointed markings on its leaves make the *Kalanchoe tomentosa*, or panda plant, as it is commonly called, pretty to grow as a house plant. As it grows older, it puts out side branches from a central stem in a bushy growth pattern.

The scientific name of the species (Tomentosa) indicates that its leaves are entirely covered with a dense matting of hairs, giving it a furry look.

The succulent lithops conforms to its name of living stones

The succulent lithops conforms to its name of living stones. Coming originally from South Africa, the 70 odd species are all similar in resembling pebbles. In some the colouring on the top of the divided 'leaves' is transparent forming windows to admit the sun to the living tissue.

The plant consists of leaves in pairs, split by a central fissure from which flowers emerge. The lithops customarily grow in clumps, as illustrated.

Cotyledon has leaves which curve upwards to catch the rain or dew

Cotelydon undulata is a pretty, bushy variety of succulent, with wavy edges on up-curved leaves. which are covered with a thick, waxy pure-white bloom that rubs off when the plant is handled. A mature plant reaches a height of 3 feet and bears orange-coloured blooms during the summer.

The name cotyledon comes from ancient Greek and means a cavity—after the cuplike leaves of some varieties, such as this one. Some 30 species have been identified, mostly natives of South Africa.

CHAPTER 3

Favourite flowering plants

Everyone loves the flowering house plants. Their fresh blooms sometimes fragrant, always colourful—catch and hold the eye of all who enter the room.

Some flowering plants are in bloom for only brief seasons of the year, others continuously. You can, if you plan it properly, have a variety in bloom all year.

On these two pages you will see a selection of the most interesting and colourful flowering house plants with which you may want to start your collection. The following pages contain more detailed information on how to grow these plus a good many others. Ever-flowering begonias and African violets head the list of those house plants which are perpetually in bloom. Geranuims will reward you with two long flowering seasons if you take stem cuttings at the correct time. Cuttings rooted in late summer bring autumn and winter blooms in addition to spring and summer flowering.

Some flowering plants bloom for only a short period which perhaps makes them more appreciated. If they flowered perpetually, plants such as the amaryllis and the spring flowering tulips and hyacinths would not seem quite as attractive as they are in their brief season.

Seasonal or perpetual, these flowering plants make an attractive and bright addition to your home.

Blooms all year

African violets are among the most widely grown of all house plants. They come in a wide colour range, purple being the favourite.

Force bulbs for an early spring

Hyacinths and tulips are favourite spring bulbs to bring into bloom indoors while it is still winter outdoors. Many other spring flowering bulbs can also be forced successfully. Buy bulbs from your florist or nurseryman from September onwards.

Tender amaryllis bulbs will bloom indoors in time for Christmas

Newer, cold-treated amaryllis bulbs take about three weeks to come into bloom, just in time for the Christmas season.

Faintly bell-shaped, their faces sometimes measure as much as 8 inches across. There are many colours including red, orange, salmon pink and white. The finest bulbs, bigger than teacups, are imported from Holland.

Gloxinias in glowing colours are favourite spring and summer blooms

You can grow gloxinias from tubers, as is shown later in this chapter. Or, if you have patience, you can develop new tubers from leaf cuttings of a flowering plant.

Once a plant comes into bloom, the buds will continue to unfold for weeks. Colours available include white, white-fringed scarlets to a deep indigo, as well as solid red.

The red geranium at the window sill provides colour and warmth

Geraniums cost so little each spring as bedding plants that, if you wish you can enjoy them while they bloom and then discard them.

Geranium growing makes a rewarding hobby, taking cuttings and collecting the varieties with distinctive foliage and blooms of many hues—the white, pinks, and reds. See later pages for instructions on methods of making stem cuttings of all varieties.

Do not confuse the geranium, properly pelargonium, with the garden geranium, or Crane's bill.

African violets

The African violet has amazing charm. It is not really a violet at all, though it comes from Africa. It grows flowers which look like violets, in violet colours of blue, white, purple, plus soft pink, with both single and double blooms, as well as ruffled. The foliage, too, differs from one variety to another. Some are more glossy, more hairy, or more quilted looking than others.

Saintpaulias, to use their correct botanical name, bloom for months on end, and are among the easiest of all house plants to propagate. If you join the Saintpaulia and House Plant Society you will be able to trade leaves with collectors throughout the country to increase your treasury of varieties.

There are some tricks to growing handsome African violets as you will learn in the following pages. Light, water and feeding are the important factors for success.

This variety grows naturally into a nosegay

Scores of new varieties of African violets have been developed over the past decade or so. This one, is particularly attractive because of its habit of putting up all the blooms at the centre, like a carefully arranged nosegay.

African violets will grow under artificial light

are the favourite plants in many homes

Good, strong electric light actually substitutes for daylight with African violets. See section on growing plants under artificial light for more detailed information on this method of cultivation. The clear lavender-blues, rosy pinks, bicolours, snowy whites, and deep reddish purples provide you with an endless variety of bloom. A big collection like this is best seen from above. Display them on a low table, so you can look down on to the plants.

*African violets like
an even temperature
and light soil mixture*

All saintpaulias like warmth and
humidity and they grow well in
temperatures of 60-70°. They
are given humidity by plunging
their pots in outer container containing moist peat or inside a
goldfish bowl. On a very cold
night, it is advisable to give some
protection to a plant on a window
sill by moving it into the room or
placing heavy cardboard between
the plant and window glass.

The best soil mixture consists
of one third each garden loam,
course sand, and of humus, leaf
mould, or peat moss.

Follow these tips for healthier plants

*They will thrive
if you give them
sufficient light and water*

An east or west facing window is
usually best for African violets, as
direct rays of sun may burn the
leaves. A north window, except
during summer, probably does not
supply adequate light.

African violets grow well under
artificial light. (*See chapter five*).
Water when the top soil feels dry,
or use a wick-type container. Keep
water off leaves as brown spots
may otherwise develop.

Good care is repaid with colourful blooms the whole year round

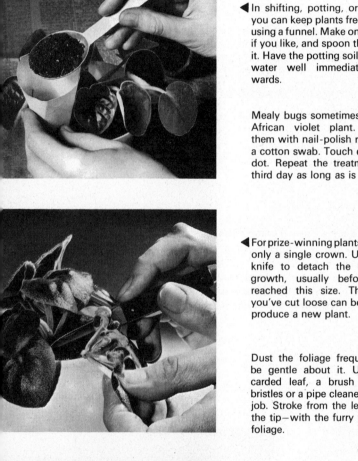

◀In shifting, potting, or repotting, you can keep plants free of soil by using a funnel. Make one of paper, if you like, and spoon the soil into it. Have the potting soil damp and water well immediately afterwards.

Mealy bugs sometimes attack an ▶ African violet plant. Eliminate them with nail-polish remover on a cotton swab. Touch each white dot. Repeat the treatment every third day as long as is necessary.

◀For prize-winning plants, you need only a single crown. Use a sharp knife to detach the competing growth, usually before it has reached this size. The portion you've cut loose can be rooted to produce a new plant.

Dust the foliage frequently, but ▶ be gentle about it. Use a discarded leaf, a brush with soft bristles or a pipe cleaner to do the job. Stroke from the leaf base to the tip—with the furry nap of the foliage.

◀Wick-style containers are ideal for African violets, since they keep the soil moist and require little attention. Use lukewarm water, add plant food to the water as directed on the packet.

The smooth edge of a ceramic pot ▶ is ideal for African violets. If using an unglazed clay pot, cover the edge with cellophane tape or dip in paraffin or shellac, to protect the leaves from harmful salts the pot soaks up.

Use a sharp knife to sever a leaf from the mother plant, with 1- to 2- inch stem attached. Choose a leaf with a firm but not a rubbery stem.

How to increase your collection of African violets

It is so easy to grow African violets that you may have to resist a temptation to grow too many. They make welcome gifts, and if you become a collector, young plants can be grown to trade for new varieties.

Leaves will root in water or sand

A healthy leaf from a mother plant will root in water, although water-produced roots are less vigorous than those grown in sand, vermiculite, or perlite and may suffer a greater setback when transferred from water to the potting soil. The pictures and instructions in this chapter illustrate both methods.

Tips on potting young plants

Whether the leaves are rooted in water, vermiculite, perlite, or sand, the size of the pot is an important consideration. Select a small pot to start with—a two- or three-inch pot at most. Young plants in too big a pot are difficult to water properly since the roots fill such a small proportion of the total soil, and it may be dry on the surface while still quite damp at the centre. As the plant grows, move it to a larger sized pot.

Not essential, but an extra assurance of vigorous roots is dipping the stem end into a root-hormone powder.

Insert the treated leaves in moistened vermiculite or a coarse sand to root. Only a small pot is necessary if rooting only one or two leaves.

If you want to start many leaves at a time, use a cake tin filled with a rooting media. Sprinkle with lukewarm water to moisten the container thoroughly. A plastic cover traps the moist air.

To root the leaves in water, cover a jar with foil or wax paper; punch holes in the top and insert leaves. They will root in 2 to 4 weeks. Then pot in a sandy soil until new leaves appear.

African violets can be attractively displayed under glass

Although African violets can tolerate rather dry air, they prefer high humidity. This is one way to provide it while also displaying the plant to advantage, and reducing the need to water it so often.

Line the bottom of a large glass or plastic globe with a 2-inch layer of sphagnum moss then lower the plant carefully into bowl and tuck in extra moss to hide pot. Keep moss damp so it will, by gradual evaporation, moisten air inside of the globe.

Because they like humidity, young African violet plants are good to include with others in a showcase. Instructions on how to plant this type of garden are given on pages 142-143.

BOWL

SPHAGNUM

When the new growth, still attached to the mother leaf, is about this size, it is ready to be moved from the original pot into ordinary potting soil.

When new plants are 2 or 3 inches tall, they may again be shifted to the next larger size pot. You can separate each rosette and plant it individually, or pot the entire clump together.

When potting plants, put a piece of broken clay pot or a bottle cap over the bottom hole to ensure drainage without washing away the soil. Hold the plant in the centre of the pot and fill round it.

Geraniums - old favourites that are now back in fashion

After years of comparative neglect when it was fashionable to decry the geranium, these plants have recently come back into favour. This refound popularity has meant that many new varieties have been developed and there is now a considerable choice available to the geranium fancier.

It is easy to see why geraniums are such popular plants. Their big heads of bloom look like gay, little umbrellas; their foliage has a spicy scent; and they are always cheerful about growing indoors in winter as house plants, then moving outdoors for the summer to brighten a porch, terrace or garden.

Geraniums like lots of sunshine

Rather undemanding plants in most matters, geraniums will not tolerate shade. Unless they get some sun each day, they grow 'leggy' and refuse to bloom. To be successful with geraniums indoors, you should place them in your sunniest window.

Temperatures ranging from 60°-70° are ideal, and plenty of fresh air and high humidity help to ensure a good display.

Never overwater potted geraniums

Potted geraniums do best when allowed to become quite dry between waterings. They are not one of the plants—like ferns—which are happy with their roots constantly damp.

When you water, do it thoroughly—until water runs out of the bottom drainage hole. Water again only when the soil is quite dry to the touch.

Geraniums benefit from regular doses of plant food when in bloom, but fertilising while they are in their dormant phase only makes plants grow overtall and spindly.

A windowful of geraniums ▶

makes a cheering sight

on a dull day

Geraniums, or Pelargoniums, to use their botanical name, come in many varieties. Colours range from the common reds to white, pink and lavender.

Most widely grown are the zonal varieties, usually doubles, although there are attractive singles, too, with solid green or variegated leaves.

Move geraniums outdoors

in the summertime

A single healthy geranium in an ample pot can bloom continuously throughout the summer. If you wish larger outdoor colour splashes, use 3 to 5 plants in 4-inch pots and sink them in the soil of a tub or plant box.

Exchange old plants for new by making cuttings twice each year

Geranium plants need regular pruning to keep them growing in a bushy, pleasing shape. The stems which are cut back can be rooted to give healthy, new plants.

Early in spring, prepare the outdoor flower bed for the cuttings taken from the vigorous plants which have been growing indoors.

After rooting the cuttings—follow step-by-step directions on the opposite page—pot them up, and set them in a sunny window. They will be ready for planting outdoors in about four to six weeks.

In late summer, take cuttings from the plants that have been flowering outdoors so you can again have blooms in the house, when your garden has gone to sleep for the winter.

Pinching back the tips helps to keep your plants full and bushy

This pink geranium is shapely and full of bloom because terminal growth was pinched back several times to achieve a low, well-branched plant. As soon as flowering stems appear, pinching should be stopped to allow the plant to go ahead and bloom. Water amply while the plant is in bloom.

Follow these steps to start geraniums from cuttings

1 Take cuttings 3 to 5 inches long, cutting or breaking between the joints, or just below where the leaf is attached to the main stem. Avoid both soft, immature and old, woody branches.

2 Trim the lower leaves from the cutting to allow for a planting depth of 2 inches. Be gentle in cutting or breaking off the leaves and cut off no more than is absolutely necessary.

3 You can get cuttings to root faster in many cases by treating them with root stimulants or hormone powders. Dip the cuttings into the powder following instructions on the packet.

4 Set the cuttings in vermiculite, perlite or coarse sand. Keep moist—not soaking wet. Keep cuttings in light but not sunny spot until roots begin to form and then move into the sun.

5 The cuttings are ready to pot when the roots are 1½ to 2 inches long—usually in 4 to 6 weeks. Sit in a 4-inch pot, providing for bottom drainage. Leave room to water at the top.

6 Pinching encourages branching on a young plant. When it is about 6 inches tall, use a sharp knife or fingertips to pinch off the tip. Failure to do this makes the stalk grow too tall.

Flowering begonias

Everblooming begonias are among the best of house plants, for they are easy to grow and reliable about putting forth their small blooms of pearly white, pink or red.

The varieties pictured here are bedding begonias, inexpensive to buy in the spring and place outdoors for the summer. They continue flowering when you bring them indoors.

Because both plants and blooms are small, they won't look at all spectacular unless you grow and show them in quantity, as in the tree arrangement pictured on the next page, or with many plants to a pot.

Grow as many as you want by taking stem cuttings from the plants you have, by the method shown below.

Everflowering begonias can be multiplied easily

Use a sharp knife to make 4-inch cuttings from a mature plant. Make the cut on a slant. Remove enough of the lower leaves to allow for inserting from 1 to 2 inches in rooting medium.

Fill a shallow wooden or metal box with coarse sand, perlite, or vermiculite. Use a pencil point to poke holes and insert the cuttings to a depth of 1 or 2 inches. The leaves should not touch.

When the cuttings have developed roots which are about 1 inch long, it is time to move them to small pots. Supply bottom drainage and fill with potting soil. Press down and water.

In a few weeks, the plant roots should fill the soil ball in a small pot. Check by tapping the pot edge against a table and remove the plant. If the roots have filled the ball, move to a permanent pot.

bloom both indoors and outdoors

Begonias will bloom
in sun or in shade

The many varieties of *B. semperflorens* do well both outdoors as summer bedding and indoors as pot plants. Some have a bright orange-red or even purple foliage as attractive as the flowers. These are the fibrous rooted types of begonia, and may be bought inexpensively in Spring from nurserymen, florists and even in many markets.

Cuttings taken from your begonia plant
can be attractively displayed on a wall tree

There is a secret to the success of this begonia 'tree'. It's the water-tight cups in which the pots of begonias stand.

These cups make it possible to water the begonia plants as frequently as necessary with no fear of streaking the wall or of water spotting the floor.

The large ceramic container is placed at the bottom of the tree, and is planted with a large number of the young plants to give a full, bushy look at the base.

Tuberous begonias
provide a spectacular display in summertime

Tuberous begonias grow best in partial shade, which makes them good choices for pots and window boxes where colour is desired.

Flower sizes run from 2 to 8 inches in some of the single varieties. In shape, they resemble rosebuds, or the smooth semi-double and double camellias. The blooms are solid in colour except for those of the Picotee type which have deeper colour in the margins of the flowers.

Partial shade, a loose, rich soil, protection from the wind, moisture in the air and soil, are the four requirements for the most success with begonias.

When the blooming period ends, tubers may be dried out, stored in plastic bags, and saved until the following year when they can be planted again for more blooms.

◀ A living pillar of bloom

A vertical plant stand of this type (several designs are available) serves a double purpose. Its decorative possibilities are obvious, lifting flower colour to eye level. But it has practical virtues too: each plant gets its fair share of the light that is necessary to its well being. Make sure pots do not dry out too quickly in a situation such as this.

Brighten a porch with begonias

Brighten your porch or entrance hall with colourful pendulous begonias hanging from the edge of the porch or from a hook on the wall. Make sure that they are protected from strong winds and from too much sunlight.

Start tubers in pots in mid-March to mid-April for big summer blooms

Small, healthy tubers will flower, although the bigger the tuber the more stems there will be. For the best effect choose tubers at least 1½ inches across. Blooms of the bush type are larger than those used in hanging baskets.

To start tubers, use 6 to 7-inch pots. Fill each to 1 inch of rim. Press the rounded side of the tuber into the soil as far as shoulder. Do not cover the dished-in top until the new sprouts are about 3 inches tall.

Group *gloxinias* for a colourful display

Success with gloxinias depends more upon proper watering than any other single factor. Test by squeezing some of the soil into a ball in the hand; if it falls apart when touched, water is needed.

Gloxinias also require a warm, moist atmosphere during growth and blooming. Put them in bright light, but not in direct sun as the foliage will dry and shrivel up.

Gloxinia's needs are similar to those of the African violet ▶

Open, porous soil, good light but not strong sun, careful watering with tepid water—all these requirements of gloxinias are very close to those of African violets.

It is also possible to reproduce them in the same fashion—by rooting leaves.

For striking gloxinia flowers start with healthy tubers

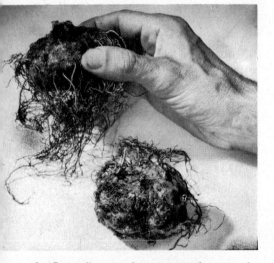

1 Depending on the source, tubers can be bought from December to April. The tuber should show dry bits of last year's growth, with pinkish new growth on top, and roots below.

3 When the new growth looks like this, lift the tuber and move to the usual potting soil. Use at least a 5-inch pot to allow for growth of roots. Handle new roots quickly and gently.

2 Avoid rot by starting tuber in vermiculite, perlite, or coarse sand. Leave the fresh tip exposed. Add water at the outer edge of the pot; do not pour into the crown of the tuber.

4 Fill the lower half of the pot with potting soil. Hold the tuber in one hand then sift soil about it. The top of the tuber should be left uncovered. Press down the soil and water.

Amaryllis has many attractive relations

◄ Modern bulbs are
treated to flower
in time for Christmas

You can buy amaryllis bulbs which have been pre-cooled to flower during the Christmas season.

For step-by-step directions on planting the bulb, caring for it during blooming and until next year's blooms are due, see the following pages.

The common daffodil
is a cousin
of the amaryllis

Daffodils grow easily indoors, either in soil or, as here, in water-soaked pebbles. When the flowers have finished, plant the bulbs in the garden. They may miss a season but will give flowers again later.

Clivia bears orange
blossoms in winter ►

Bulb-like but not a true bulb, clivia, or Kafir lily, blooms once a year, but its foliage is evergreen.

Plant and care for it as for an amaryllis except that the drying-off period should be omitted.

On page 2, there is a colour picture which shows the true beauty of this plant in bloom.

There is a blaze of colour
when amaryllis bursts into bloom

Blooms appear rapidly after you plant an amaryllis bulb—some within 21 days. Their big trumpets of colour are especially rewarding in a season when showy flowers are few. Choose from several tones of red, orange, salmon, or solid colours striped with white.

Four simple but important steps to follow when planting an amaryllis bulb

1 Size is important: the bulb on the right is too small; buy those which are $2\frac{1}{2}$ inches in diameter or larger. The bulb should have some roots attached, and *may* show new growth at the top.

2 Supply bottom drainage. Use a pot (6-inch or larger) big enough to leave an inch of space free round the bulb. Place the bulb so that half of it is above the soil level. Preserve all roots.

3 Leave an inch of space free at the top of the pot; water until excess drains out of the bottom, using lukewarm water. Place the pot in a warm sunny window, preferably facing south.

4 Flower buds have a little indentation or dimple at tip—like the one the pencil points to. If night temperature drops below 60° in window, move the plant to a warmer spot for the night.

They will bloom, year after year

Care for the plant when the flowers fade for healthy blooms next season

A bulb uses up its food reserves in producing flowers, then regains its strength through leaves and roots to make the next year's bloom. You can help the process with plant food. Use a dry or liquid form. Follow the directions on the packet.

As soon as blooms wither, cut off with a razorblade or sharp knife, flush with stalk, so that no stub remains. This prevents the possible formation of seeds which would only rob the bulb of its strength. Continue watering and keep the plant in the sun.

The stalks begin to turn yellow shortly after the last flower fades. When this happens, they can be removed without making the plant 'bleed'.

Cut off the stalk where it emerges from the bulb, being careful not to injure the leaves or bulb.

When frost danger passes, choose sunny outdoor location for the plant. Dig a hole that is deep enough for the pot rim to be level with the surface of the soil, first placing some gravel at the bottom of the hole to guarantee good drainage.

Water and feed through the summer. Lift before the frost and store dry in basement for 2-3 months. Bring to the light again and water. As the bulb has not been cold treated, it will revert to its normal time of blooming—late winter.

Forced bulbs bring an early spring to your home

◀ *Deceive spring flowering bulbs*

By a process known as 'forcing', i.e. bringing to bloom at an earlier date than normal, these daffodils and crocus were coaxed into flowering indoors far ahead of those outdoors. The following pages tell you how to do it.

Hyacinths, daffodils and tulips ▶

are easily forced bulbs

The larger the bulb, the simpler it is to force. Especially with the early varieties of these bulbs. The later the bulb blooms outdoors, the harder it will be to force it successfully indoors.

1

To succeed in forcing, it is important to plant healthy bulbs firmly in good soil or bulb fibre. Give enough water to dampen the soil.

2

In warm areas, delay planting till the cold weather. Soil temperatures should be below 48°, but the bulbs should not freeze.

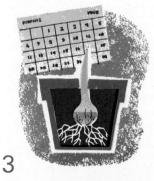

3

Allow at least 8 weeks of cold weather to pass before you lift the pots and bring them indoors to 60° cool room temperatures.

4

Make sure roots fill the pot and that tops are several inches tall before bringing pots indoors. Check the roots to be certain.

Forced bulbs should be planted outdoors first

Sink spring bulbs outdoors for three months and then bring them indoors to bloom

1

Sit the bulbs in pots so that their noses are just below the pot rim. Do not overcrowd. Press the soil down with your fingers, and water.

2

Put the pots in trenches with the rims 1-2 inches below the soil level. Stakes and labels help to locate and identify the pots later.

3

When the shoots are 1-3 inches tall, bring the pots indoors. Keep them dark, at no more than 60° for a week; then move them to a sunny window.

Hyacinths are favourite ▶

bulbs to force

There are hyacinth bulbs on sale which flower indoors if grown in water. There is a greater danger of bulb rot with this method of forcing than if bulbs are sunk in soil outdoors, and brought indoors to flower.

Flowers last longer if the plant is removed from bright sunlight before flower heads are fully opened.

◀ *Golden daffodils and*

deep purple crocus

make a good colour contrast

You can depend on King Alfred daffodils to force easily. Put several in a pot for show.

Crocus isn't quite so certain to force satisfactorily. It is best to bring the pot into the light as soon as you lift it from the trench. Keep it cool for a week before putting it in a sunny window, just as with bigger bulbs.

From the time you plant spring flowering bulbs in your garden until they bloom, a period of 4 to 8 months elapses. By forcing the bulbs, you can cut that time in half.

To succeed in this method, the various stages the growing bulbs pass through must be shortened. They are: (1) autumn planting (in pots sunk outdoors); (2) prolonged cold weather (this period is reduced to 8-12 weeks in forcing); (3) warmth and sunshine to bring the buds to flower.

When planting, supply bottom drainage. Use bulb pans (shallower than the standard pots) if available. Plant the bulbs as shown in the sketch on the opposite page.

Select a site for your outdoor trench where the sun reaches it, softens the soil, and makes it easy for you to lift the pots when the proper time arrives. A southern exposure is best for this reason.

It will also be easier to lift the pots without breakage if you line the trench with dry leaves or straw before sitting the pots in it. Then cover with another protective layer before filling the trench with soil.

Do not sink pots too deep. Rims should not be more than a couple of inches below level of the soil. Heap up raked leaves over top of trench for extra protection and keep the leaves from blowing off by laying a board on top.

After at least 8 weeks of cold weather have elapsed, lift a pot and check to see if roots have formed and shoots are up, before bringing bulbs indoors to force.

Move pots first to cool room (or location where temperature is not above 60°) for a week. Keep them watered and away from light during this period. Then bring to a sunny window and watch buds swell and flowers open.

How to make your gift plants last

Delight over a blooming plant can turn to keen disappointment if you don't know how to give it proper care. And you can feel quite resentful—unjustifiably so—if you mistakenly assume that all plants should live on indefinitely, as do many foliage plants.

Some of the seasonal flowering plants must be looked upon as if they were cut flowers— to be enjoyed while they last, and to be discarded when they fade.

A number of those we traditionally give and receive cannot live long except under greenhouse conditions—so different from the desert-like atmosphere that characterises most of our homes in winter.

With a few exceptions, seasonal blooming plants will last longest in your home if you give them a cool, bright setting and plenty of water at room temperature. It takes lots of water and sometimes some fertiliser to produce blooms, and the plants should be examined every day to determine their water requirements.

You may like to toast your legs over a hot fire, but most plants shrivel in such a setting. Blasts of cold air are equally unwelcome, so choose a spot away from cold draughts.

Do not let all these cautions prevent you from using flowering plants as decorations in places that are unsuitable as permanent homes. Just remember to move the plant back to a more congenial position when it has served its temporary purpose as a centrepiece or table decoration.

An unusual combination
of pale blooms and marbled leaves

When you buy a cyclamen plant from your florist it may have only five or six blooms showing, but look down into the heart of the plant and you will see dozens of tiny buds.

They will all push their way up and bloom if you give the plant a sunny window and lots of water. In this, it is an exception to the general rule that seasonal, blooming plants last longer out of the sun. Pour water in at the pot edge, not into the crown of the plant.

Increasingly popular, these ▶
Christmas red poinsettias

New, longer-lasting varieties of the vivid poinsettias (*Euphorbia pulcherrima*) are available in greater quantities in this country now. The scarlet bracts surround the small and insignificant yellow flowers in the centre. White and pink varieties are also obtainable. Keep warm, out of draughts, well watered, and they will last through the holiday season.

Plants will last longer if

Check daily to see that the plants are obtaining sufficient water

◄*Winter Cherry plant has bright orange fruit which resembles cherries*

There are more than 900 species of the solanum, but only a few varieties can be forced into fruit for winter decoration indoors. Good light and plenty of moisture at the roots are necessary for its continued health, and an occasional light spray with tepid water helps to provide the humidity it requires. Even with the most careful treatment it will seldom last more than a few weeks indoors unless enabled to have an occasional rest in a warm greenhouse.

A bloom-laden azalea will flower for weeks ►

Keep your azalea plant in a good light but in a fairly cool spot if you want it to last as long as possible. It will probably need to be watered each day. Examine daily to make sure.

Once it stops blooming, resign yourself to discarding it—unless you live in an area where winters are mild. In this case, sit it outdoors in spring, treating it as any shade-loving shrub.

◄*Winter flowering begonia gives you lavish amounts of bloom*

Many types and colours of winter flowering begonias have been developed, some of which can be maintained in flower throughout most of the year. Usually sold here as named hybrids, the plants like warmth and plenty of water. Keep out of draughts and regularly remove all withered flowers for continuity of bloom.

protected from blasts of hot or cold air

CHAPTER 4

Move potted plants outdoors in summer

A summer out of doors is of real benefit to most house plants. Nearly all like the brighter light they can get on porch, patio, or in the garden. But not all like direct sun, as do the geraniums and coleus pictured here. Others need protection also from strong winds and beating rains.

Follow the advice on the following pages in choosing the outdoor position which is best for your favourite house plants.

Big pots of blooming geraniums ▶
convert any spot to a flower garden

In a tiny back yard, most of its surface covered with concrete, a few pots of bright geraniums produce a colourful show.

Geraniums will not flower freely unless they get lots of sunshine. Pinch back ends before the blooms come on to get a bushy and shapely plant.

Coleus plants should be moved into the garden in summer

Because they need a lot of sun, coleus plants grown indoors are apt to become 'leggy' quickly. If you break off the tops, they root easily in sand or water.

Take stem cuttings early in spring from house plants and have them ready to set outdoors as soon as the warm weather arrives. Sink the pots as shown, or set the plants directly into the ground.

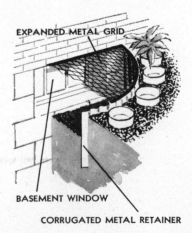

EXPANDED METAL GRID

BASEMENT WINDOW

CORRUGATED METAL RETAINER

Potted plants can be displayed outside in tubs or borders

There are two ways to do this. The simplest way is to buy healthy young plants from your florist or nursery in Spring. For a good summer display, group several in a large pot or in the garden.

If you have space indoors, preferably a large sunny window-ledge, you will also enjoy the other way—taking your own cuttings in early spring. When warm weather arrives, you then have a crop of young plants ready to be planted.

There are several house plants which can be easily propagated by cuttings. Geraniums, coleus, everflowering begonias are among the most obliging. Chrysanthemums can be rooted this way, too, but success is less certain.

Brighten a shady spot

Rose-rainbow coleus plants and everblooming begonias make brilliant companions for edging plants like exacum used here in a partly shaded spot. Take cuttings at the end of summer to carry indoors.

Geraniums in pots make patches of colour

Fill in gaps in a flower border with portable colour—geraniums in pots. Striking containers do much to enhance the simplest of plants and make them suitable for sophisticated surroundings.

Rewarding plants in many colours ▶

Petunias, pansies and geraniums are all strongly coloured and give lavishly of their flowers in summer. They are very easily grown and require relatively little attention. You only need to ensure that they have sufficient water and drainage is adequate. Feed them regularly and snip off every bloom as it withers in order to ensure a continuous display of rich and varied colour.

These plants are particularly effective when displayed in borders or tubs as shown in the illustration.

Change the scene when you wish with pot gardens

Give tuberous begonias a prominent setting ▶

The luxurious appearance of tuberous begonias is displayed to best advantage when pots of them are hung on a garden fence. Begonias should receive direct sun only in the mornings.

After you move the plants outdoors, use a fine spray to water them, and remember that they need to be watered frequently.

Potted plants can fill the gap between outdoor flowering seasons

Once the spring bulb show is over, the average garden looks a bit bare until summer blooms come along. Fill in the gap with potted plants like these to brighten a garden wall. Have colour where and when you want it.

◀ Shaded sunlight is perfect for many of your foliage plants

A back-yard fence like this one which is equipped with staggered shelves to accommodate potted plants has many virtues.

It gives protection from wind and too much sunlight; it makes the most of a small amount of space and it masses plants so that they take on importance.

Almost all of the ferns, vines, and common foliage plants you grow indoors in winter would find such a setting as this ideal for the summer months.

Your plants will benefit from a summer outdoors

The outdoor life is as appealing to most house plants as it is to people during the summer months. House plants appreciate extra sun, and so you can leave them outdoors most of the time as long as they are protected from too much harsh sunlight and strong winds.

Indoors, it is almost impossible to give them all the light and humidity they need for a long and healthy life. If they spend their summers outdoors, they will store up enough energy to last a long time under less than perfect indoor conditions.

Use discretion in choosing a position. Give the more fragile plants a summer home on a shaded porch or in a wall niche like the one pictured at the top of the page. Others, like geraniums, succulents and cactus, will revel in the sunniest spot available.

Make a plant box to match the fence

Both the plant box and fence are of stakes. Into the box is set a row of house plants, still in their clay pots. Because it is a sunny spot, graceful ivy and bright geraniums are the best choice. If you want to copy the idea in a shadier place, try ferns and philodendrons.

Have a garden at your doorstep

A rustic garden bench is twice as inviting in an outdoor sitting area because of the plants grouped around it. It takes only a few to give a true garden atmosphere to a paved, outdoor area such as this.

The same sort of treatment — wall brackets for climbing plants, tubs for upright ones — would work equally well on a porch or balcony.

◀ *Place a row of potted plants along the garden path*

This is an idea to appeal to any city dweller with limited garden space and a liking for plants.

Set a row of pots along a garden path—with a fence serving as a background and windbreak—to create the impression of a garden planted in the usual manner.

Caution: remember that plants in pots dry out quicker than ones growing in the ground.

Cactus and succulents like a season in the sun

Shallow saucers—a Japanese idea—make good showcases in which to display a collection of cactus and succulents outdoors.

Their root systems are so shallow that no damage will result if you unpot them and plant them in the different containers. Repot to bring indoors in the winter months.

Protect big plants

Summer winds can be surprisingly strong. If you intend to place a large plant outdoors, ensure that it has ample protection from the weather.

Placing the plant next to a fence is wise. A heavy tub for a container is further guarantee against its being toppled and broken.

Succulents *flourish where it is hot and dry*

Massed succulents
make a colourful display

Sedums in bloom are set in the foreground, kalanchoes in the centre, and 3-foot-tall cotyledons at the back of this group.

Succulents revel in sunshine and well drained soil. Never allow roots to paddle in accumulated rain water. Many grow in shallow soil and will spread happily on a wall, sometimes overflowing from pots in which they have grown during winter.

◀ Little care is necessary
with this endless variety

Small, beadlike-leaved sedums come in a bewildering number of varieties. They are eye-catching for colour and formation.

Echeverias in rosette shapes put up graceful flowering stems during the summer months.

Unless it rains very infrequently, you probably will not need to water them at all. Be sure the pots they grow in have adequate bottom drainage. Place them in a bright and sunny spot.

Succulents look best ▶
in groups

Single plants in the succulent family may be unimpressive. In a group—easy to achieve if the plants are in pots—the effect will be striking.

Echeverias, sedums, agaves, and aloes are some of the heat-loving succulents shown here.

Be sure to bring tender succulents indoors well in advance of winter weather, as one light frost could wipe them out.

Plant boxes
put colour where you want it, indoors or out

The plants you set outdoors for the summer will look more handsome and will be simpler to shift if they are grouped in a plant box.

Indoors, too, it is often advantageous to move plants about—from where they are placed permanently to where they can obtain some extra sunlight.

Inexpensive to build, a plant box similar to those pictured here requires no expert carpentry. It can be made by anyone who is handy with a hammer and saw.

Metal strips trim a simple timber box

The box of simple construction timber is rectangular in shape. Its polished metal corners give it an indoor look. The casters with which it is equipped make it move easily, even when the box is loaded with heavy pots!

When you build your own plant boxes, you can modify the dimensions to suit your needs

1 This box is made from 1-inch thick timber, 12 inches long by 30. The bevelled 12 x 8 base is recessed to take the casters.

2 Coat the metal, handles and sides at once with plastic sealer as a protection against tarnishing and discolouration. Waterproof the inside of the box.

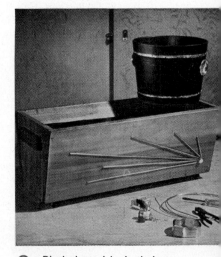

3 Black plant tub is plastic, long lasting, easily cleaned and virtually unbreakable. Many sizes, shapes and colours are available.

Use a shovel as a skid. Best on grass and smooth surfaces.

Heavy sacking or canvas make good slings for a move across paving.

Rustic style plant box is suited to outdoor living

Scored wood panelling is used for the body of this box, with plain wood trim. It is being moved into place by rolling along paved surface of terrace on three sections of pipe.

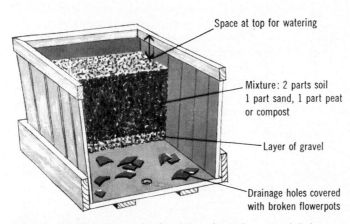

Space at top for watering

Mixture: 2 parts soil 1 part sand, 1 part peat or compost

Layer of gravel

Drainage holes covered with broken flowerpots

Success with plants grown in plant boxes depends on good drainage, correct soil mixture, and care in giving the proper amount of water.

Borrow the youngsters' trolley for long hauls. Planks add extra width.

'Egyptian carry' works if you have a helper. Use rope, 2 x 4s.

An old pair of roller skates supplies mobility. Saw off the heel flanges, and remove the front clamps. Bore holes in the platform of each skate and bolt to cleat underneath.
  Paint the inside with Solignum or other wood preservative to protect the wood from moisture. Allow paint to dry and fumes to disperse before filling with soil.

To move short distances, use pipe lengths and rotate from front to back.

Detailing enhances the basic plant box

This box looks graceful because of the trimming and careful attention to details. Diagonal kerfs and concave indentations give it a professional look. Directions below how to build one like it!

For one important plant to decorate a terrace or patio, use a tub big enough to be noticed and sturdy enough for its outdoor setting. Any of the four pictured here will be suitable.

Whatever style of outdoor plant box you decide to build, follow these general rules to ensure good looks and healthy plants:

(1) Mitre all outside corners for a neat look and a tight fit.

(2) Raise the box so that air can circulate under it and protect it against mildew and rot.

(3) Sink all nailheads and fill with putty.

(4) Sand all corners and edges smooth.

(5) Paint inside of box with Solignum or other suitable wood preservative.

(6) Bore holes in bottom and spread a 1-inch layer of broken flower pots on the bottom before you sit plants in place. This will guarantee good drainage.

Basic construction is simple and detailing can be added with a power saw and drill

Use timber 1¼ inches thick by 12 inches wide; 1-inch timber is too thin. Taper sides to 11-inch base, and mitre to fit. Or, use butt joints and metal angles to brace the joints.

The sketch on the right shows how the scrap timber and dowel provide steady pivot point while the concave cut is being made. You need four dowels, 2½ inches long, one for each side.

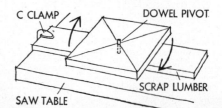

After tapering sides, cut shallow kerfs on the diagonals as shown. Do this with a small chisel if you prefer to have wider kerfs.

Drill a pilot hole for the dowel in the middle. Then, in a piece of scrap wood, drill another hole to accept dowel which is serving as a pivot.

With the pivoting jig in place, rotate sides on dowels; turn down the setting on the saw as you cut. Remove the dowel, coat with glue and re-insert as plug.

Good designs for an outdoor box

For a new look, try a hexagonal box

Sturdy frame gives grip for fingertips

This is a plant box large enough to accommodate plants with a big root system. The top facing adds a finished look and provides a convenient surface on which to sit pots or tools while working.

Before planting, coat the inside of the box with a water-proofing material. To take care of drainage, start with a 1-inch layer of gravel; add another inch of gravel for each 6 inches of soil it takes to fill the box from this point to the top. Fill the rest of the space with equal parts of gravel, garden loam and peat moss for a healthy soil mixture.

For a six-sided box, start by drawing a pattern of a perfect hexagon on paper—as in the diagram shown on the left. Transfer to wood and cut out the base.

Cut side pieces to fit the base. Fasten with nails or screws.

Outer strips trim an inner framework

To make this square plant box, use a mitre box to saw the ends of the facing strips at a 45-degree angle. Assemble and attach to a square base.

Space 1 x 2-inch strips $\frac{3}{4}$ inch apart, and nail to inner framework.

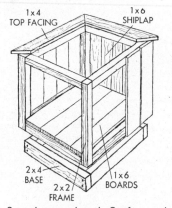

Saw 12 2 x 2s to the same length. Set four uprights as pillars. Nail the rest in between, top and bottom, to form a rigid frame. Nail on bottom planks, cover with shiplap or other timber as you prefer. Set plant box on a recessed pedestal made with 2 x 4s.

CHAPTER 5

How to grow
healthy plants

Light, soil and water—these are the three factors that determine the health of your house plants. Requirements for each of the three elements vary from plant to plant, but the combinations are neither so great nor so mysterious as you may think if you are a beginner at indoor gardening.

Once you know that most of the foliage plants we call 'house plants' are natives of tropical forests, you understand why they flourish in a subdued light—as if filtered down through leafy trees—rather than in full sun that scorches tender leaves.

For the same reason, these plants prefer moisture in the air (though many are extremely tolerant of the near-desert conditions that prevail in our homes in winter), and moist, porous soil resembling the forest loam where their ancestors once took root.

The drawing below charts how a plant manufactures its food from the soil, water, light and air that are its environment.

In the pages to follow, you will find basic information on light, soil and water requirements of average house plants, plus specific data on special needs of favourites.

Choose the right plant

Consult the table on the facing page for help in selecting the plants which will grow best in the home conditions you can offer.

If you have no sunny windows, you had better leave out geraniums. If you want a vine in a dimly lit spot, grow rhoicissus rather than an ivy with variegated leaves. If you have had bad luck in the past, pick an 'easy-to-grow' plant that can thrive in less than perfect growing conditions.

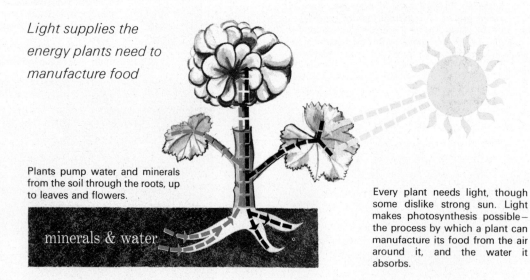

Light supplies the energy plants need to manufacture food

Plants pump water and minerals from the soil through the roots, up to leaves and flowers.

minerals & water

Every plant needs light, though some dislike strong sun. Light makes photosynthesis possible—the process by which a plant can manufacture its food from the air around it, and the water it absorbs.

FLOWERING PLANTS

PLANT	HEIGHT	LIGHT*	SPECIAL NOTES
African violets	to 6 inches	medium	Use porous soil mixture. Keep cold water off leaves.
Amaryllis	20-30	high	Plant high in pot. Give sun and food after flowering.
Begonias	6-24	high	Grow fast, need repotting oftener than most house plants.
Spring flowering bulbs	6 upwards	high	Need 8 to 12 weeks of cold. Keep dark until well sprouted.
Geraniums	6-18	high	Many varieties. Allow soil to dry out occasionally.

FOLIAGE PLANTS

PLANT	HEIGHT	LIGHT	SPECIAL NOTES
Aluminium plant	8-15	medium	Pinch to keep thick. Spray with water in dry weather.
Bromeliads	2-10	medium	Have small root systems—will grow well in small pots.
Dieffenbachia	to 60	low or medium	Leaves tip-burn if humidity is low. Avoid draughts.
Ferns	6-20	medium	Use a light soil mixture with lots of organic matter.
Monstera	tall	low or medium	Also called cutleaf philodendron. Moist atmosphere best.
Palms	6 upwards	medium	Grow well in low light if given a good moisture supply.
Peperomia	6-12	low or high	Many varieties. Need light, well-drained soil.
Rubber plant	tall	any exposure	Sensitive to overwatering. Air layer when it gets spindly.
Schefflera	tall	low or medium	Grows best when kept on the dry side in a warm room.

CLIMBING PLANTS

PLANT	HEIGHT	LIGHT	SPECIAL NOTES
Ivy	—	high	Likes humidity high, drainage good, occasional sun bath.
Kangaroo vine	—	medium	Semi-trailing. Give care similar to that for African violets.
Rhoicissus	—	low	Tolerates low light situations very well.
Philodendron	—	low-medium	Many varieties. Extremely adaptable. Grows in water or soil.
Scindapsus	—	medium	Sometimes mistakenly called variegated philodendron.
Syngonium	—	medium	Grows upright while young; twines as it grows older.

EASILY GROWN PLANTS

PLANT	HEIGHT	LIGHT	SPECIAL NOTES
Aspisdistra	tall	any	Called 'cast-iron' plant for its hardiness. Grows slowly.
Coleus	6-12	medium-high	Many colours; brighter if in sun. Roots easily from cuttings.
Crassula	6-24	medium-high	Keep on the dry side. Old plant becomes treelike.
Pandanus	tall	medium-high	Thrive in sunny, dry, hot situations. Do not overwater.
Chlorophytums	—	any	Trailing plant; roots from offsets. Tolerates low light.
Sansevieria	6-20	any	Withstands adverse conditions of low humidity and light.

* For more detailed information on light requirements, see following pages.

Watering

Moisten all of the soil

When you water from the top, add enough water so that it drains out at the bottom. You can then be sure that all the soil is moistened. Use a saucer to catch drainage, and protect the surface on which the plants are placed.

Wick-water from bottom

Special self-watering flowerpots have a built-in reservoir that feeds water to soil through a wick. Make one with a fibre glass wick, a disc to hold pot above water and a deep dish to hold water.

All beginners, when growing plants indoors, ask how often they should water their plants. The correct answer, 'That depends . . .' is not as satisfying as some definite reply like 'once a week' might be. But it is the only accurate reply.

Your home in winter may be almost as arid as a desert, and your plants will need far more water than during humid summer weather. Small pots dry out more rapidly than big ones, and so must be watered more frequently. Plants in bloom need more water than at other times.

But, in general, plants vary little in their water requirements. Except for cactus and succluents, which tolerate drought, all plants grow best in moist soil.

Add water whenever the top soil feels dry to the touch—whether this be daily or weekly. When you water, do it thoroughly. Supply enough to moisten soil all the way to the bottom. Do not water again until top soil is on the dry side.

Top versus bottom watering

The diagrams on the left show you two satisfactory ways of watering. If you water from the top, be sure to have broken crockery, pebbles or other loose material at the bottom of the pot for good drainage.

If you water from the bottom, do not use drainage material. Insert a wick (preferably of fibreglass) to absorb water from a dish below and to keep the soil uniformly moist. You can also buy self-watering pots in a variety of styles and sizes.

Whether you water from top or bottom, it is a good idea to give plants an occasional soaking. Place the pot in a dish or pail of water so that it is half submerged. Leave it there until the surface of the soil is moist. Set the plant aside and drain off the surplus water before returning it to its usual position.

Do not leave a pot standing in water more than an hour or so. Too much water over a long period prevents oxygen reaching the roots which need oxygen to live.

Feeding

A little plant food goes a long way—too much may burn the roots and actually kill a plant. The various brands of fertiliser on the market differ in their strength, so follow exactly the directions on the package.

Older plants benefit from a light feeding every two or three months, except during the winter, when it is best to feed somewhat less frequently. New plants obtained from your florist need no fertiliser for the first six weeks after you get them, or even longer.

Commercial fertilisers always tell on the packet the proportions of nutrients they contain. Those usually present are nitrogen, phosphoric acid, and potash. When you see the figures 5-10-5 or 10-6-4, it is to the percentages of these elements, and in the order stated above, that reference is made.

When should you fertilise?

It is unwise to assume that any sickly looking plant will benefit from a dose of plant food. The plant is much more apt to be ailing because of too much water, too little light, too dry an atmosphere, or the poor quality of the potting soil in which it is growing.

If your plant is suffering from starvation, nitrogen is most likely to be what it lacks. Symptoms are a yellow colour in new leaves, and lack of vigour in new growth.

However, symptoms of injury from gas fumes, too much water or too little light are similar, except that when one of these is the culprit, lower leaves usually turn yellow, while those higher up stay green.

Dry plant foods come in powdered, granular and tablet form. You can also buy plant food as a liquid. Experiment with various types to see which gives you the best results.

When you use dry food, be careful not to spill it on the plant, and to water it into the soil at once. Tablets may be inserted into the soil at the outer edge of the pot, and will be absorbed gradually in the course of successive waterings.

The main thing to remember about fertilisers is always to follow the directions given.

Measure food accurately

Water dry food into soil to prevent burning. It is usually best to make a solution of a dry fertiliser with water. Apply commercial food exactly as the packet directions state.

Tips on liquid fertiliser

When you use liquid plant food in solution, be sure to measure the water just as accurately as you do food. Pour in the liquid until the excess drains out of the bottom of the pot.

Light

Houses are built for people—not plants. By a plant's standards, they are too dark, too dry and often too hot—like sunless deserts. The wonder is that so many plants survive.

The light requirements of plants have have received careful study by scientists in recent years, and the indoor gardener has benefitted from the results of their research.

The chart at the bottom of this page shows you how little light is actually available in places where house plants are grown. The tables on the facing page group plants by minimum amounts of light needed if they are to prosper. Compare the two and you will see that most plants just do not get enough light.

Effects of too little light

What happens when a plant gets too little light? Nothing, at first. Plants can survive for rather long periods on reserve food. But ultimately, the new growth becomes spindly, the new leaves smaller and the lower leaves die.

It may take only a few weeks, or as long as a year for a plant to show symptoms of light starvation. The cure is not a massive dose of light—which could kill a plant—but a return to adequate light conditions.

Nor is it wise to set foliage plants next to unshaded windows which face directly into the sun. Very few foliage plants can tolerate direct sunlight, especially when it is magnified by clear glass. Shifted to such a position from a dim corner, the sun will burn them.

There are several ways you can give your plants more light: by moving them closer to windows, by moving them to brighter rooms and by leaving curtains and blinds open during the day. But the most convenient way is to supplement natural with artificial light.

You may use either incandescent lamps or fluorescent tubes to supplement sunlight. Spotlights, too, have been successful, and are decorative as well as functional.

Fo a more complete discussion of growing plants under artificial light, see the pages on that subject later in this chapter.

Determining light intensity

Charts and tables on these pages show you light measurements in terms of foot-candles. If you are a camera enthusiast, you will be familiar with this term which appears on light meters. Use yours, or borrow one, to make an accurate check on light in your home in places where you grow plants.

Lacking a light meter, you can calculate light intensity roughly if you know that at 500 foot-candles, you'll see a shadow outline cast by your fingers when your hand is placed between light source and plants.

Judge the light a plant gets from these typical readings

HOMES

General illumination	5 foot-candles*	
Reading or writing	20	,,
Ironing and sewing	40	,,
Workbench	40	,,

HOTELS

Reception Hall	20 foot-candles	
Dining Room	5 to 10	,,

OFFICES

Typing, accounting	50	,,

Conference Room   30 foot-candles

STORES

Circulation areas	20 foot-candles	
Merchandising areas	50	,,
Displays	100 to 200	,,

OUTDOORS

Bright summer day
About 10,000 foot-candles
Cloudy winter day
500 to 2000   ,,

*Amount of illumination at all points from a uniform point source of one international candle.

Plants are listed by minimum light needs for 16 hours a day

Need 15 to 25 foot-candles minimum

LOW LIGHT

Aglaonema
Araucaria
Aspidistra
Calathea
Cissus
Dieffenbachia
Ferns
Sansevieria
Several philodendrons

Note: the darker the leaves the less light is required

Need 25 to 50 foot-candles minimum

MEDIUM LIGHT

Aechmea
Aralia
Billbergia
Bromeliads
Dracaenas
Ficus
Ivies
Maranta
Monstera
Peperomias

Note: the darker the leaves the less light is required

Need 50 to 100 foot-candles minimum

HIGH LIGHT

African violets
Begonias
Cacti
Coleus
Crotons
Chrysanthemums
Geraniums
Hyacinths
Poinsettias
Saxifraga

All flowering plants have high light requirements

Potting and

1

Use ⅓ gravel for drainage; ⅓ peat to hold water and nutrients; garden or other soil makes up remaining third of a well-balanced potting soil mixture.

2

After putting in coarse material for drainage, press the soil gently around the tender roots. When the pot is full, firm the soil down and leave room at top to water.

3

Water the newly potted plant thoroughly. Sit the pot where it receives light, but not strong sun until after it has become adjusted—two or three days.

Proper potting gives plants

a good start in life

Whether you begin with a seedling, a rooted cutting, a plant lifted from the garden, or a bulb, how you first pot a plant is vital to its future health.

Most important of all is the quality of the potting soil in ·which your plant is to grow. With few exceptions, all house plants thrive in potting soil composed of gravel, peat, and soil in equal proportions—as illustrated in the top drawing on the left.

You may make up your own potting soil mixture, or buy it commercially prepared. But whatever kind you use, be sure it is moist—not dry or wet. Tender roots 'settle in' best and suffer least damage in moist soil. It's handy to keep some that's properly damp in a plastic bag, ready to use whenever it is needed.

Standard John Innes soil composts, for seeds or more mature plants, can be obtained from most garden stores, florists and some chain stores. These mixtures are made to recipes devised by scientists at the John Innes Research Institute, and do not vary.

Do not forget to put a layer of coarse material for drainage in the bottom of the pot before you begin to fill with potting soil. Broken chunks of clay pots or small rocks are satisfactory for this purpose. Omit this step if you are using one of the self-watering pots.

Finally, if the plant is young and is expected to grow rapidly, allow for this future growth in selecting the size of the pot.

Clay pots come in sizes up to 14 inches. Standard size has a depth equal to top diameter. Bulb and azalea pans are shallower.

Ceramic or plastic pots without a drainage hole need a bottom layer of a coarse material to provide good drainage.

Quantity of potting soil needed to fill standard 4 inch flowerpot is 1 pint; for a 6 inch pot, 3 pints; for an 8 inch pot, 2 quarts.

re-potting

Repotting older house plants stimulates healthy growth

A plant needs repotting when its roots become matted around the outside of the soil ball in which it is growing. Fast-growing plants should be examined every 3 or 4 months. Slow-growing plants may not need repotting more than once a year.

Normally, it is best to shift a plant to a pot no more than an inch or two larger than its former pot. If the pot is too large in relation to the plant, the soil will dry out very slowly and it will be difficult for you to control the moisture—the top soil may be very dry while the central soil is still wet.

The roots of a pot-bound plant need not usually be disturbed at all when you put it into a larger pot. Merely add more potting soil to the bottom, sides and top.

If the original soil ball has become packed down, has poor drainage, or too many soluble salts (from hard water), then all of the soil should be removed and replaced. Do this gently, so as to damage the roots as little as possible, and spread roots as you sift fresh potting soil around them.

Beginners worry about damaging plants in the course of repotting, but this is really a simple operation to perform without injuring a plant. Water the day before repotting so that all of the soil ball will be slightly moistened. Then follow the three steps pictured on the right to give your plant room for new and vigorous growth.

Clean pots thoroughly before re-using. Steel wool makes quick work of removing encrustations from inside or outside of pot.

Sterilise soil mixture if you believe it is infected. Bake moist soil mixture at 250° for $1\frac{1}{2}$ hours in a closed container.

Rule of thumb dictates the amount of space—a thumb's width—you should leave free below the pot rim to allow for water.

1 To remove the plant, place fingers over the soil ball and turn the pot upside down. Tap on a table edge and the plant will slide out. Repot if roots are matted.

2 Cover hole in pot with a bottle cap or bit of broken pot to keep the soil from washing out. If pot is over 4 inches deep, a layer of gravel will improve the drainage.

3 Sit the plant in the new pot to test height. Add soil to bring to correct height. Fill around roots with soil and press firmly with thumbs. Water and keep out of the sun.

Adventures in greenhouse gardening

Once you become an enthusiastic gardener, you will want a greenhouse of your own—whether is is a sizeable private paradise like the one pictured across the page, or a miniature portable model like the one which is sketched below.

In winter months, there is nothing to equal the exhilaration of watching plants bloom in a greenhouse, while the weather remains bleak and frosty. Foliage plants, too, luxuriate in the warm, moist atmosphere a greenhouse can provide.

Types of greenhouses

Lean-to greenhouses (see sketch on the right below) are popular because they can be attached to houses of almost all types and ages. They come in prefabricated form (as do larger, free-standing ones) or they can be a 'do-it-yourself' project.

Other types of attached greenhouses are the half-span and even-span, jointed to the main building by metal flashings. The even-span greenhouse exposes more glass to the sunshine and is easier to erect.

In choosing the position for the lean-to type of greenhouse, you will find the southerly side of your house best—where it receives the most light. Morning sun is important; late afternoon sun is negligible.

Next to sunshine, heat and ventilation are most essential. You may be able to attach a greenhouse heating outlet to equipment you already have, or you may prefer to invest in one of the compact, efficient heaters built for the purpose. Your local heating-equipment dealers can help you decide about this.

Do not build too small a house. It is difficult to ventilate and heat small areas under glass: temperature climbs rapidly when the sun comes up, and drops almost as quickly when it goes down or is blocked by clouds.

Ample ventilation by sashes in the roof and sides is also a neccessity. A large opening or doorway into the house to which the greenhouse is attached is a great help—it cuts down heat-absorbing wall space and provides an extra volume of air to cushion against rapid outside changes of temperature.

The most satisfactory way to ventilate is by means of a thermostatic control which automatically opens and shuts vents when the temperature rises above or falls below the desired degree of heat.

A good masonry foundation which is sunk well into the ground gives the best protection against severe frost.

Greenhouse preview of spring

This lean-to greenhouse is part of a recent re-modelling and joins a family room made from a two-car garage. The floor of the greenhouse is sunk 18 inches, letting you look down on the flowers.

Greenhouse gardening can be done on any scale—large or small

Portable indoor types have glass or plastic tops and sides. Orchids and all plants can be grown from seed. This one includes the fluorescent fixture to supplement the sun. Sit on a stand or table.

Lean-to greenhouses in prefabricated models may be bought in kit form—all parts are cut to the exact size and shape you want. Attach to south wall if you can.

Indoor gardening under artificial light

You can grow luxuriant house plants anywhere in your home with the aid of man-made sunshine—electric light. Corners so dark they'd discourage even a cast-iron plant can be turned into good settings for the light-loving varieties by using the proper amount of artificial light.

Most plants get too little light during the winter months, not only because of the low light intensity, but also because the day is so short. To remedy this, the perfect winter situation for a house plant would be in daylight by day, with a boost from artificial light during both daylight and dark hours.

But there are many plants which will live and thrive for varying periods of time on nothing but artificial light, in amounts the average indoor gardener can supply at a moderate cost. African voilets, begonias and gloxinias are some that will reach impressive proportions without ever catching a glimpse of the sun.

Positions for lighting

Enthusiasts for gardening under artificial light have placed their equipment all over the house—from living room to basement, even in cupboards! But if you intend to grow a large number of plants, and experiment with propagation from seeds and cuttings, your basement or a spare room will perhaps be the best location. It will offer ample space and a lower temperature—probably from 55°–65° —which is better for most varieties of house plants.

Also, young plants not yet ready for showing are out of sight until they reach a stage where you want to bring them into the public rooms of your home for display.

You can, of course, start on as small a scale as you wish—one plant under a table lamp. If you use an incandescent bulb, have at least a 75-watt bulb, placed no more than four feet from the foliage and no closer than two feet. A fluorescent tube, because it gives out less heat, can be placed closer to plants.

There are many possible variations that will work well and be decorative, too. Try an enclosed plant case, such as the one pictured across the page, or some of the other equipment sketched and described on following pages. All can be built by a handyman at moderate cost and operated economically.

You can use either incandescent or fluorescent lights for this kind of gardening. Experiments show that a combination of both fluorescent and incandescent light is better than either used alone. It is beneficial to supplement with some incandescent light, particularly when a 'daylight' type of fluorescent tube is to be used.

Research studies indicate that a plant will live and stay attractive for at least a year if it is lighted 16 hours daily with the minimum light intensity it needs. The list at the bottom of the page groups plants according to their minimum light requirements in terms of foot-candles per day. For further listings and discussion, see the pages on light earlier in this chapter.

To reduce your work, you may wish to install an inexpensive automatic timer which will turn lights on and off as needed, without your having to remember them.

Some plants that can be grown under artificial light

700–1000 foot-candles
Achimenes
Beloperone guttata (shrimp plant)
Clivia
Coleus
Croton
Fuchsia
Gloxinia
Impatiens
Kalanchoe
Sedum
Winter cherry

300–700 foot-candles
Hoya (wax plant)
Kangaroo vine
Maranta (prayer plant)
Pilea (artillary plant)
Saintpaulia (African violet)

25–300 foot-candles
Philodendron varieties
Sansevieria species
Scindapsus
Syngonium podophyllum

Two 40-watt fluorescent tubes supply energy for growing plants in a plant box with a lath drainboard at the bottom. Short plants are raised up to the same height as tall ones.

A garden under artificial light becomes a boxfull of colour when the lid is raised

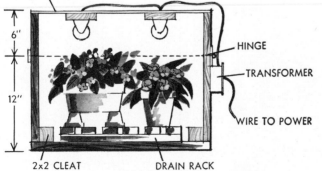

1/8" HARDBOARD TOP

6"

12"

HINGE

TRANSFORMER

WIRE TO POWER

2x2 CLEAT

DRAIN RACK

Cross-section view shows how plants are raised up so all are same distance from light. Both cuttings and plants need 16 hours daily from two 40-watt tubes.

5'

24"

35"

2x4 LEGS

1x4 BRACE

Painting interior of box white increases light intensity. Hinged lid can be raised to control the humidity and temperature.

*A basement plant box is easy
to build and maintain
in a small amount of space*

If you use this unit for starting cuttings and seedlings, you can increase its efficiency by providing bottom heat. To do this, you can use a standard heating cable—such as is used in hotbeds. The cable should be thermostatically controlled, at an even temperature of about 75°.

With the unit closed, the uniform temperature will make control of the humidity easier. In an open unit, the effect of bottom heat on humidity would be difficult to evaluate.

Your local electrician will advise you concerning the installation of the heating cable and thermostat.

*Grow flowering plants, root cuttings and seedlings with an
Economical light-bench combination like one shown below*

Folding trestles, waterproof pans of 24-gauge galvanised metal, lights on pulleys and a metal reflector create a winter garden. If using 85-watt fluorescent tubes, place them 12 inches above plants; 60-watt incandescent bulb lights an area 4 x 4 feet if suspended $2\frac{1}{2}$ to 3 feet above plants. In either case, use the light 16 hours a day.

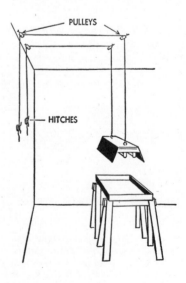

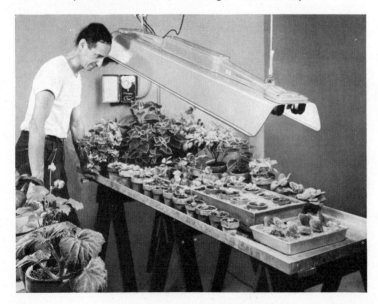

Lighting arrangements for your home

Here are four arrangements for growing plants under artificial light. Those across the page are for a basement or seldom-used room, where looks are unimportant. Those on this page are attractive enough for anywhere in the house.

Any of these arrangements may be modified in dimensions to suit the space you have. All will interest any indoor gardener who has more plants than window ledges, or few well-lighted spots.

If you want to grow seedlings and cuttings in quantity, you'll probably want to copy one of the constructions on the facing page, since they give you maximum space at minimum cost.

These two installations are equipped with bottom trays of waterproof metal or plastic which you can line with sand or sphagnum moss. By keeping the bottom layer moist, you can reduce the frequency with which you'll need to water. Also, evaporation from bottom layer will increase humidity of air surrounding plants. The air of an average home is too dry for most house plants, and they will be healthier in this atmosphere.

To reduce your work in operating any of these arrangements it will be worthwhile installing an automatic timer.

Lighted plants can be used as a room accent

This plant cabinet is both functional and decorative. The sliding glass doors give it a humid, greenhouse-like atmosphere, and keep plants dustfree.

Shelves are staggered (see the cross-section view on the right) so that all plants can benefit from the light tubes which are placed in the top of the case.

The heat generating transformer for light tubes is outside the cabinet. Bottom vents keep moisture from fogging glass doors.

To reduce watering, use self-watering pots, or insert a wick in each pot which will soak up water from the metal tray holding several of the plants.

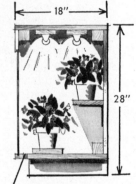

VENT HOLES

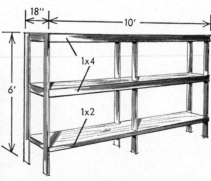

This wall-rack arrangement is suited to a family-room where plants will get some daylight, with artificial light as a growing boost. Construction is simple, and measurements may be altered to suit the space available.

Terrarium showcase for your plants

Like an oasis in a desert, a tiny, moist world of growing things inside a glass terrarium has an irresistible fascination. The glass garden invites you to paint your own scene, imitating nature on a miniature scale.

The dry, hot air of the house in winter is no handicap to plants in the terrarium where moist air is trapped. Since moisture is so well conserved, a glass garden needs little water once it has been planted. An occasional sprinkling when the surface soil feels dry to the touch is all that is necessary.

Preparing the container

Wash and polish the container so it will sparkle. Then place charcoal, gravel and soil as shown in the diagram below. A lining of moss, green side out, between the soil and the glass is attractive.

A good soil mixture is 2 parts loam, 2 parts coarse sand, 1 part leaf mould—not so rich that your plants will rapidly outgrow their rather limited space.

Before you plant the terrarium, decide where you wish to display it. If it is to be seen from one side, put larger plants at the back, smaller ones in front. See the list below for plants that like a humid atmosphere.

Use the glass lid of your terrarium to control humidity and watering. If moisture condenses, remove the cover for a time. Place your glass garden in good light, but not in strong sunlight, for this would trap too much heat and kill the plants.

Plants suitable for a terrarium

Begonias (everblooming)
Baby's Tears
Fittonia
Helxine
Ivy (miniature types)
Maranta
Palms (small)
Pteris (table ferns)
Peperomia
Saintpaulia (African violet)
Wood plants: evergreen seedlings;
   dogtooth violet, Dutchman's breeches;
   dicentra; hepatica; varieties of
   mosses; mushrooms.

Garden in glass keeps plants glossy and green in moist air

Leave cover open for air

Use glass cover

Soil

Taller plants at rear

Line sides with moss

Small plants at front

Charcoal

1 in. of gravel

Choose slow-growing plants for your container, and don't plant too thickly, or they will soon crush one another. Cuttings planted directly in a terrarium will quickly form roots there.

For an effective arrangment

place the most interesting plants

at the front of the terrarium

Use your imagination when you choose plants to arrange in your glass garden. Make miniature hills and valleys by mounding up or scooping away the earth.

Try to place each plant so it will present a pleasing contrast of shape and colour with its neighbours—variegated foliage next to the solid, colourful next to green, and so on.

Remember that half the charm is the small scale effect. As plants grow too large, replace them with cuttings or plants of correct size.

Learn how to recognise plant diseases

Sick plants are easily cured once you know the cause of trouble

1 LIGHT

If your plants are getting too little light, they may not show any ill effects for a short period of time. They will continue to produce new leaves by using stored energy.

If light is insufficient for a longer period, new stems become spindly. The foliage gradually becomes yellow-green and eventually all growth stops and the plant dies.

To cure light starvation, move the plant to a sunny window or give it an extra amount of light artificially in the evening. For plants in stationary plant boxes where you know light is consistently insufficient, it is wise to install an overhead light to supplement whatever day-light reaches them.

Plants in the home seldom get an overdose of light. If they've been accustomed to filtered light, rays of direct sun will burn them. Or, if you place them close to a window, the glass can intensify the heat enough to do severe damage to tender leaves. Too much sun produces burned spots on foliage.

Different plants require varying amounts of light. In general, the foliage plants can survive with considerably less light than those which produce flowers. Choose the proper plant for the light situation you can offer and you'll have few light troubles.

2 PLANT FOOD

Plants manufacture their food from the air and the soil in which they grow by a process called photosynthesis, in which light is the source of energy. Fertilisers supply essential minerals, of which nitrogen is an important one and often unavailable in sufficient quantity for healthy growth. If there is too little food, the new leaves may be smaller than normal, and perhaps will be lighter in colour. Growth will be slow, and both stems and leaves will be smaller than usual. To cure this, adopt a regular feeding programme for the undernourished plant.

You can use the same fertiliser that you put on your lawn. Or you can buy fertilisers especially made for house plants. They come in powder, liquid, or tablet form. Follow the directions carefully.

If there is too much food, applied accidentally or carelessly, the roots of your plant may be burned. The plant will then wilt even when the soil is moist.

To cure this trouble, flush extra plant food out of the soil with lots of water, or repot it in fresh potting soil.

Don't assume that every plant which looks sick is in need of a quick dose of fertiliser. Make sure that the trouble is not due to some other cause of poor plant health.

3 WATER

If a plant receives too little water, it will wilt. This seldom causes serious damage unless it occurs frequently, and then it stunts growth and causes flower drop.

Too much water is more common. The first symptom is usually the dropping of lower leaves. New leaves may continue to appear on top, but an overwatered plant gets leggy and bare of foliage at the base.

If you suspect that a plant has had too much water, tap it out of its pot and look at the roots. Root tips should be white. If they are brown, repot in loose, spongy soil mixture and water less frequently.

Moisture in the air is also important to a number of house plants. It is difficult to supply adequate amounts under average winter home conditions, where air is consistently warm and dry. If there is too little humidity over a period of time, the leaf tips of some plants will turn brown.

You can increase the amount of humidity in the immediate vicinity of the plants if you grow them in a metal plant box or tray lined

and how to treat them

with pebbles. Sit pots on these and keep them moist. Evaporation will increase the humidity of the air layer just above and surrounding the plants.

If you use this method, you must not have water deeper than the pebbles, for drainage action through the bottom hole of the pot must continue to take place. If the pot stands in water, the roots will receive less oxygen and they will rot, just as when you over-water a plant from the top. Alternatively stand the pot inside a larger container and pack peat between the two, keep this always moist but not wet.

4 PESTS, DISEASES

Plants grown indoors will seldom be attacked by insects or disease if you buy them from a reputable florist or nurseryman.

The only disease—as distinct from infestation by insects—which occurs often enough to consider here is caused by soil-borne, rot-producing organisms. In young plants, it is known as 'damping off'. In older plants, it is called 'stem rot'. As there is no effective remedy, a plant which has this disease should be destroyed promptly.

Those insects that attack house plants can be controlled with the same chemicals used to eliminate similar pests outdoors. An aerosol house-plant spray is both effective and convenient to use indoors. Follow the directions carefully.

To prevent any pests from getting a hold, clean plants regularly by syringing them in the sink, or by cleaning their foliage with a soft, damp cloth. The water you use should be lukewarm. Support each of the leaves by holding the palm of your hand under it as you wipe the top clean.

Even with good care, pests occasionally gain a foothold. If they do, isolate the infested plants until you've destroyed the insects, so that healthy ones will be protected.

Frequent cleaning, regular examination, and prompt treatment eradicate insects

Give them a warm bath in soapy water

Supplement monthly washing or wiping of foliage with a twice yearly thorough cleaning in soapy water.

Red spiders and mealy bugs are controlled by this type of treatment, followed by an application of an insecticide over the plant.

For scale, scrub the leaves gently with a soft brush and then apply insecticide.

Check regularly for signs of insects

When you examine a plant, turn the leaves over and look at their underside—where most insects are active in their work.

The group of mealy bugs shown on the right can easily be eradicated by a thorough sponging, followed by spraying with an insecticide. Isolate the plant from the others.

Treat promptly to eliminate scale

Protect plants from heavy scale infestation like this by inspecting them often.

Early treatment will prevent serious damage and is more effective than late attempts to cure the trouble.

To treat scale, purchase a spray designed specifically for that purpose. Read the label on the spray and follow instructions.

Care for your plants regularly to achieve best results

Good grooming for house plants is essential if you want them to serve as attractive ornaments for your home.

Make it a practice to inspect each plant whenever you water it. Insects, suspicious-looking spots or holes in the foliage, should be noted and the plants isolated in order to begin treatment.

If the foliage looks dusty, carry a soft, damp cloth and wipe each leaf or take the plant to the sink and syringe it with a fine spray of lukewarm water.

If the plant is taking on a sprawling pattern of growth, or going to seed, pinch back the ends of branches and remove yellowing or unattractive foliage to give a tidy, compact appearance and encourage new growth.

None of these jobs takes more than a few minutes. But if they are performed regularly, they will greatly improve the appearance of your favourite house plants.

A quick, convenient means of combatting almost any pest that attacks house plants is the handy 'aerosol' insect spray. No mixing is required; and there is no cleaning afterwards.

Follow the manufacturer's directions exactly for best results.

Cottony-white mealy bugs are a common house plant pest, with the African violet as the favourite victim. Dilute white spirit with equal parts of water; use a toothpick wrapped in cotton to touch each insect with the solution.

Sterilised soil or a John Innes mixture should mean you get no soil pests. If you use garden soil and gnats, beetles, ants or other pests appear use some of your garden DDT or a nicotine spray to clear them from your indoor pots.

More tips on pest control, training and grooming

When climbing plants grow large, they look better grown on a support. Ivy has been trained to climb a trellis, just like the one for a rose, only smaller. Make one the size you need and paint it to match the colour of the foliage.

Encourage the plant to put out new shoots by pinching off some of the end growth. Reroot and plant cuttings in a pot if growth at the base seems sparse.

Remove the blooms from all flowering plants as soon as they begin to wither. Do not let them go to seed and waste the plant's energies. Some, like the coleus opposite grows a flower shoot which should also be pinched off to improve the attractiveness of the plant.

Keep your plants clean and they will grow better and look better. A soft, damp cloth makes the best duster for the big-leaved plants like this fiddleleaf fig.

Support each leaf from the back with one hand and dust it gently with the other.

If the leaves show water spots, sponge with a mild detergent solution. Rinse with lukewarm water.

Hairy-leaved house plants, such as Rex begonias, or gloxinias may either be washed with a lukewarm spray or brushed to remove dust.

A pipe cleaner or small soft-bristled paintbrush is a very satisfactory cleaning tool. Brush gently toward tips of leaves.

Any plant too big to be moved to the sink will benefit from an occasional complete shower bath as a supplement to the regular dusting of its foliage.

Use a bulb spray or a hose attached to the kitchen sink. Always use lukewarm water as cold water spots the leaves.

CHAPTER 6

How to multiply your plants

By seed

Stem cutting

Leaf cutting

Asparagus fern
Avocado
Bromeliads
Cactus
Coleus
Crossandra
Gloxinia
Impatiens
Kalanchoe
Monstera

Aglaonema
Christmas cactus
Coleus
Crown of thorns
Dieffenbachia
Dracaena
Fiddleleaf fig
Ivy
Kangaroo vine
Impatiens
Peperomia
Rubber plant
Syngonium

African violet
Cissus*
Gloxinias
Kalanchoe*
Peperomia
Philodendron*
Rex begonias
Sansevieria
Scindapsus*
Sedum varieties

* Cutting must include leaf
   bud as well as leaf

Everyone who develops more than a passing interest in house plants wants to try his hand at propagating new ones. The excitement of watching a cutting take root and grow into a mature plant never wears off.

The commonest and easiest way to increase the majority of true house plants is by a stem cutting. There are few which do not respond to this method.

Second most frequent is division. If a plant sends up a number of branches at the surface of the pot—such as the fern—it can probably be cut into several portions, and each part potted singly, as a new plant.

Growing house plants from seed—in contrast to plants for the garden—is the least used method. Once the seeds have germinated, it is difficult in ordinary home surroundings to supply the degree of humidity needed or to keep soil temperatures high enough. But for anyone who can overcome these obstacles, it is an inexpensive way to grow plants in quantity.

The plant lists below set out the best ways to propagate each plant. In a number of cases there will be several ways. The various methods are explained in detail later in this chapter.

Division

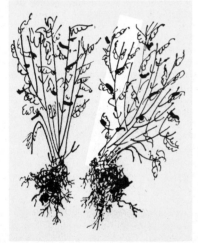

African violet
Aglaonema
Aspidistra
Begonias
Bromeliads
Echeveria
Maranta
Nephrolepsis
Pandanus
Sansevieria
Saxifrage

Runners

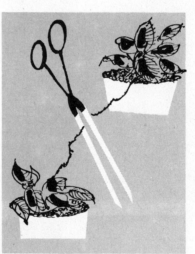

Saxifrage
—Or by offsets:
Any plant which you can
start by division

Air layering

Dieffenbachia
Dracaena
Fiddleleaf fig
Rubber plant

Soil mixture and equipment you will use to grow new plants

Starting new plants indoors can be done on a small or large scale, depending on the space you can devote to it and the number of new plants you want. A single clay pot accommodates a number of cuttings or seeds. For quantity, a seed pan is more satisfactory.

Basic care is the same

Whatever method of plant propagation you choose certain rules apply. Start with clean, strong parent plants. Don't try to root diseased, insect-infected cuttings. If you are beginning with seeds, use the best quality you can purchase.

Use clean pots or seed pans and fresh rooting materials. Don't re-use sand or vermiculite which have become infected.

Keep the rooting mixture moist, never wet, and have humidity as high as possible. Use glass lids or plastic covers to trap moist air. Dust with captan if disease starts.

A light soil mixture is best

Pot each cutting separately as soon as it has formed good roots. Use a light soil mixture consisting of equal parts of sharp sand or gravel, peat, and garden soil. Add compost to the mixture if it's available. Don't feed new plants until growth starts.

A set of small hand tools is convenient if not essential to the indoor gardener. The pointed tool included in this group is a dibber handy for making holes in the soil to take cuttings.

A pencil, kitchen spoon and fork make good working substitutes for such a set.

Here are all the basic ingredients needed for rooting and potting new plants. The plastic sheet can be formed into a tent or cover to keep humid air about seedlings or stem cuttings while they form roots.

Plastic and sphagnum moss are also used for air layering.

Use vermiculite (or perlite) or coarse sand for rooting cuttings.

Combine peat, soil, and sand or gravel in varying amounts to suit the particular needs of the new plants you are growing.

Wooden trays are practical for large-scale propagation

Normal size for seed boxes is 14 inches by 8½ inches by 3 inches deep, but any convenient size will do so long as the box is not too deep. Bottoms are normally made of 2 or 3 slats with small spaces between them. These permit efficient drainage, but will allow soil to drift through unless covered with crocks or gravel. Use only fine soil, preferably screened through a sieve.

For a small number of seeds, use a clay pot with a glass cover

Because insufficient humidity is the greatest hazard in successful germination of seed grown indoors, a glass lid or plastic cover is helpful.

Small seeds need no soil cover and may be sprinkled directly on surface of fine-screened sphagnum moss. They germinate best on a damp surface.

Wick watering or watering from the bottom is advisable so as not to disturb or wash out the fine seedlings.

Bottomless plant bands make it easy to move young plants

Good for growing seedlings up to a size where they are ready to shift into small pots, plant bands let you move young plants with minimum disturbance of tender roots.

Fit the bands into the box; fill with soil mixture and sow seeds. Pull out all but the strongest seedlings from each of the plant bands.

This same arrangement is also practical for starting a large number of tuberous begonias indoors.

You can make your own plant bands from milk cartons.

Seeds quickly grow into plants

Increasing plants by seeds is among the most dramatic and rewarding methods of propagation. Given light, warmth, moisture, and the passage of time, tiny seeds sprout, take root, grow into young plants, at the least possible cost.

Growing new plants from seeds

Plant seeds in a porous and well drained soil

◄ You can use sphagnum moss, vermiculite, perlite or soil-sand-peat mixture for starting seeds. Moisture, proper aeration, good drainage, and a sterile planting mixture are vital to young plants.

Even fresh seeds need disease protection ▶ before planting. Dusts for this purpose are available at garden supply stores. Use amount shown on knife for one packet.

*Seedlings will need to
be transplanted and spaced apart
once they start to grow*

1 Soil for seeds should be fine and free of lumps and weed seeds. If using compost or garden loam, it is best to sift it through a screen before combining with peat and sand.

2 Provide for bottom drainage. Fill container with moistened growing medium. Shake to settle. Tamp down with a brick to leave $\frac{3}{8}$ inch room at top rim for watering.

3 A ruler or piece of lath is handy for marking off rows in your box. Space rows about $2\frac{1}{2}$ inches apart. Very small seeds may be scattered on the surface.

4 Drop seeds in rows $\frac{3}{8}$ to $\frac{1}{2}$ inch apart. If growing several varieties in one box, use plant stakes to identify. Sift sphagnum moss or sand over planted rows of seed.

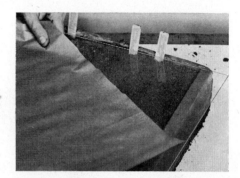

5 While seeds are germinating, keep the box covered with glass or plastic and paper to simulate darkness. Leave crack for circulation of air. Move to sun as sprouts appear.

6 As plants grow, thin out weaklings to promote development of sturdy ones. A pencil or dibber makes a good pry for lifting seedlings without damaging the roots.

7 When the first leaves appear, transplant to another container. Make a hole in the soil with a dibber so that the tender roots can be set in place easily. Water well.

Propagation by
stem cutting

Ivy is only one of many house plants that can be reproduced by stem cuttings

A plastic bag traps humidity

Wilting can be avoided by enclosing pot and stem cuttings in a plastic bag during the time when they are taking root.

Hold the bag in place with a rubber band which can be removed and replaced easily if the cuttings require water.

1 Roots develop best just below the point where a leaf joins the stem. Make your cut there. Cuttings should be from 4 to 8 inches long. Remove bottom leaf or two so as to have about 1½ inches of bare stem to insert in the rooting medium.

2 Fill a clay pot with damp vermiculite, perlite, or sand, Treat the ends of cuttings with a root hormone powder if desired. Place the stem ends in a rooting medium. Water and keep in cool spot in bright light, but not in direct sun, until rooted.

3 After about 3 weeks remove one cutting to check root root development. Growing time varies, but it should not take more than 5 or 6 weeks to produce roots of this size—large enough to warrant transplanting to a separate pot.

4 Choose the correct size of pot—not over 4 inches for a single cutting. Supply bottom drainage. Spread roots and fill in with potting soil. Even if the plant normally requires sun, it is advisable to keep it in the shade.

Propagation by *leaf cuttings*

Root leaf cuttings in water, sand, vermiculite or perlite

Cover a jar with foil or wax paper and pierce holes to accommodate leaf stem. In water, roots form in from 3 to 6 weeks, though not as rapidly as in sand, vermiculite, or perlite.

When the roots are well established—as in picture—transfer the leaf cutting to standard potting soil. New growth will appear, and the original leaf will eventually wither away.

Big-leafed begonia and some other plants can be rooted from leaf sections. Cut so that each unit includes a part of the main vein. Cut off the tips to reduce wilting.

When rooting in sand, vermiculite, or perlite, about $\frac{1}{3}$ of the cutting should be submerged. Check root formation as for stem cuttings and transplant when roots are established.

Another kind of leaf propagation

Choose a prominently veined begonia leaf with a 1-inch stem and insert stem in sand. Anchor leaf in place, face up, with toothpicks.

Use a sharp knife to sever each of the main veins. Cover with plastic film until the new plants develop at points where veins have been cut; repot new plants in soil.

Propagation by *dividing* roots

House plants may be divided any time, but spring, when new growth is about to begin, is most favourable

Division is one of the least complicated ways to increase a collection of plants. It consists merely of separating an existing plant into two or more sections, and then potting each part individually.

Any plant that grows in clumps and has a separate root system for each of its parts below the soil can be divided into two or more portions. Whenever a plant belonging to this group is in need of repotting, decide whether to shift it or divide it.

If the plant appears overgrown and solid, it will almost certainly benefit from division.

Consider at all times the well-being of your plants. The two plants, at right in the picture above, are just reaching an attractive size—they may be divided, but they will not benefit from it. But the three on the left will look better—and grow better—after dividing. Follow the three steps below to give older plants a new lease of life, or to get a new crop of your favourite house plants.

To remove the plant from the pot, turn it upside down and give the pot rim a quick sharp rap on the edge of the table. Soil ball should slide out with no difficulty.

Shake the soil from the roots so that you can see where the stem joins the main plant. Choose sections with good roots of their own which you can separate from the old plant. Pull the sections apart gently, or cut apart with a knife if necessary.

Plant new sections in the same way as for any of your house plants. Use porous potting soil, firming it about the roots. Water thoroughly. Keep in the shade for a few days.

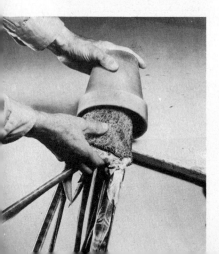

Propagation by
runners

*Plants that send out
aerial runners with new plants
forming at their ends are easily grown*

Some house plants, like this saxifrage, form new plants on runners. To get a plant to root, you just pin the runner to moist soil in a small pot placed nearby.

Roots will form quickly in a light mixture containing lots of peat and coarse sand. Keep the soil continuously moist; in a few weeks new roots will have become established, and you will be able to cut the runner.

Propagation by
layering

*Use the process of air-layering
when plants lose their
bottom leaves*

Cut a vertical notch in the stem of the plant that is to be air-layered, at the point where you would like new roots to grow. Wrap in very moist sphagnum moss and hold in place with polythene sheeting.

In four to six weeks, moss ball will be filled with new roots. (Make sure that moss remains moist; add water if necessary.) Cut off below the roots and pot. Keep the old plant. It will produce a new top if you continue to water.

Glossary of the Plant Forms

Bloom. In addition to the common meaning of a flower, this word is also used to describe a whitish substance on the leaves and stems of a plant which rubs off on handling.

Boxes. Shallow boxes for growing seedlings.

Bract. A leaf like part associated with flowers and sometimes inaccurately called a petal, as in the poinsettia and shrimp plant.

Blublike. Plant which bears some resemblance to a bulb but is not a true bulb.

Compost. Organic matter made up of fermented or decomposed materials, such as leaves, grass.

Crown. Point at or just below the soil surface where stem and root join.

Cut back. To cut or pinch off growth at tips of plants, to encourage development of side growth.

Cutting. Any part of a plant that is used to propagate new ones—leaf, stem or root.

Damping off. Disease of seedlings caused by several fungus parasites. Seedlings wilt and topple over and appear to be water soaked.

Dormant. The rest period of a plant or bulb, during which growth ceases or slows down.

Dry off. Process in which soil is permitted to become so dry that foliage is dropped and plant becomes dormant; used with many bulbs.

Established plant. Plant which is well enough rooted to take hold and thrive without intensive or extraordinary care.

Force. To make a plant bloom before its natural season of blooming has arrived.

Germination. The first growth of a seed.

Humus. The decomposed organic material which is capable of holding large amounts of plant nutrients and moisture. Usually added to garden soil and sand to make a potting mixture.

Leggy. Said of a plant which is tall and does not branch as it should, and which often has no leaves except at its top. This condition is usually caused by lack of pinching back at the proper stage of growth, or by too little light.

Lobe. Portion of a petal or leaf that divides the whole to about its middle.

Midrib. The main rib of a leaf which is a continuation of the leafstalk.

Node. Point on stem from which leaves branch out.

Offset. A short side shoot which is used for purposes of propagation.

Palmate. Lobed, divided of ribbed in a manner which resembles a hand; dias of a leaf.

Pinch back. See 'cut back' above.

Plunge. To lower a potted plant into water or a large container holding peat so that the pot is almost entirely submerged.

Pre-cooled. The term describing a commercial process during which bulbs are stored at controlled temperatures, for fixed periods, to induce flowering at an earlier than normal time.

Pricking out. The first transplanting of seedlings from original seedbed into other boxes or into individual pots.

Propagate. To increase plants by such methods as division, cuttings, or from seed.

Runners. Thin wiry shoots that a plant sends out, which produce new plants at their ends.

Shift. To take a plant out of its pot and replant it in a larger sized pot.

Slip. A stem cutting taken for the purpose of propagating a new plant.

Standard potting soil or John Innes soil composts. As used in this book, a potting mixture consisting of one third each of soil, sand or gravel, and peat moss.

Sterilisation. Treating soil in order to destroy organisms in it.

Tamp. Lightly firm down fresh soil with the hands or with a flat utensil.

Tendril. The slender prolongation of a leaf or stem which clings to a support.

Transplant. To remove a plant from the place where it is growing and move to new location.

Tuber. Swollen underground stem which bears eyes, such as potatoes.

Variegated. Including more than one colour; having a dappled appearance.

Whorl. A group of three or more leaves of flowers appearing at one node, in a circle.

Syringe. To wash a plant by means of a fine spray-covering foliage.

Wick-watering. Watering of pots or boxes from the bottom by means of cloth or fibre glass wicks inserted in soil and extending downwards into a water reservoir beneath.